RECORDED VERSIONS GUITAR

AUTHENTIC TRANSCRIPTIONS WITH NOTES AND TABLATURE

MEGADETH TH1RT3EN

C000088557

Music transcriptions by Pete Billmann, Jeff Jacobson, Paul Pappas and David Stocker

ISBN 978-1-4584-2167-8

HAL•LEONARD® CORPORATION
7777 W. BLUEMOUND RD. P.O. BOX 13819 MILWAUKEE, WI 53213

In Australia Contact:
Hal Leonard Australia Pty. Ltd.
4 Lentara Court
Cheltenham, Victoria, 3192 Australia
Email: ausadmin@halleonard.com.au

Visit Hal Leonard Online at
www.halleonard.com

Sudden Death

Words and Music by Dave Mustaine, Dave Ellefson, Chris Broderick and Shawn Drover

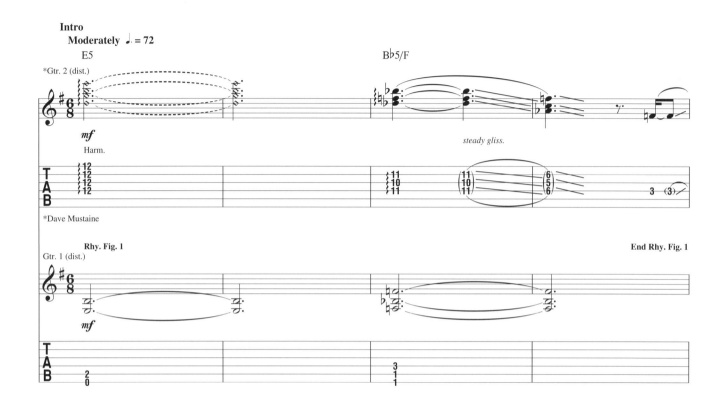

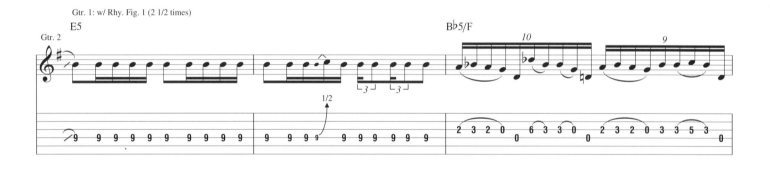

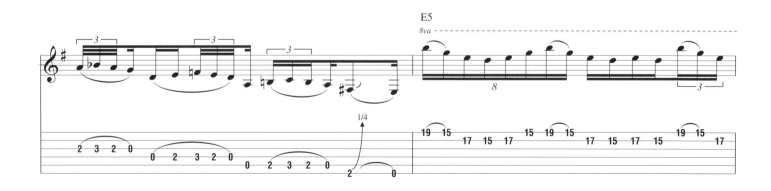

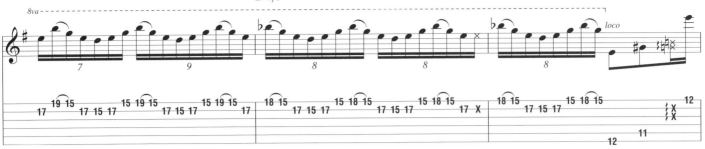

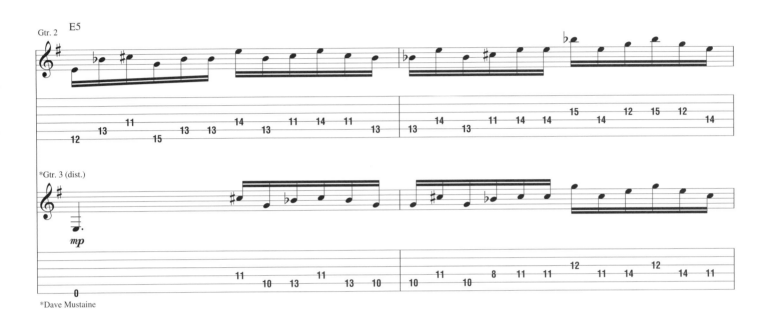

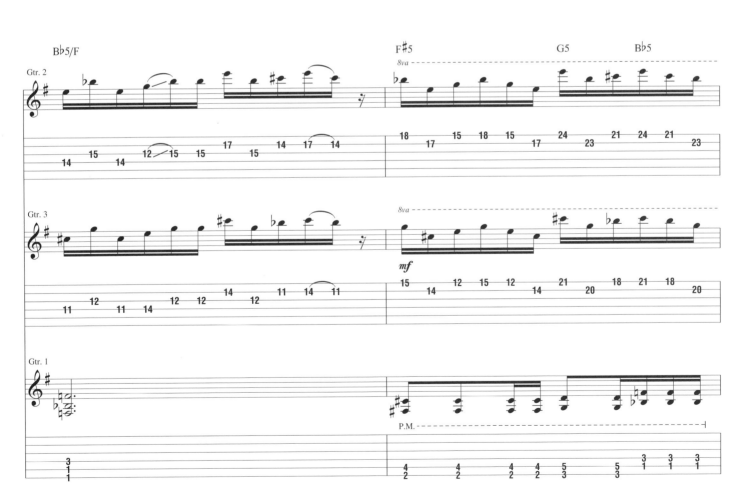

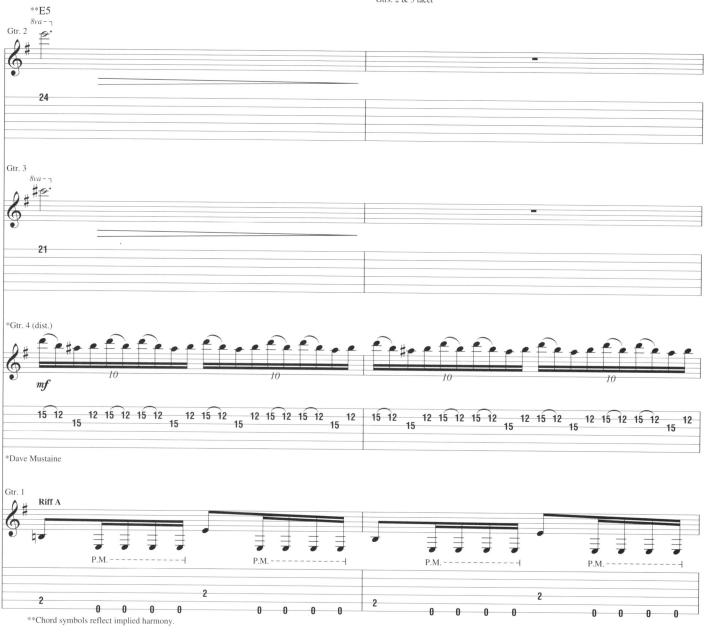

*Dave Mustaine

**Chord symbols reflect implied harmony.

4

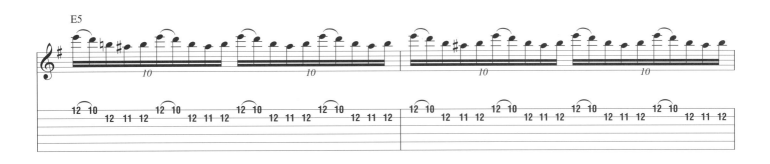

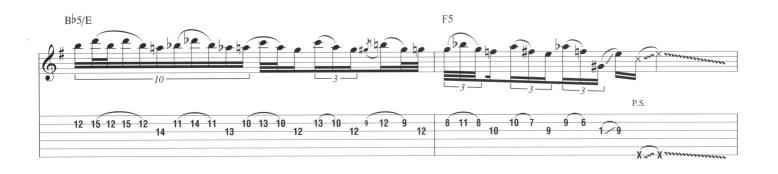

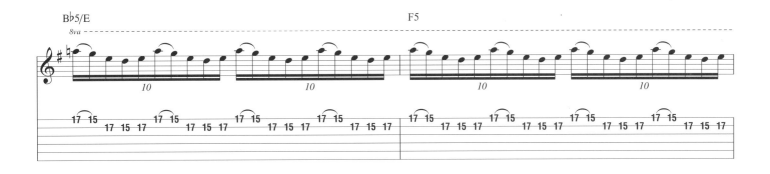

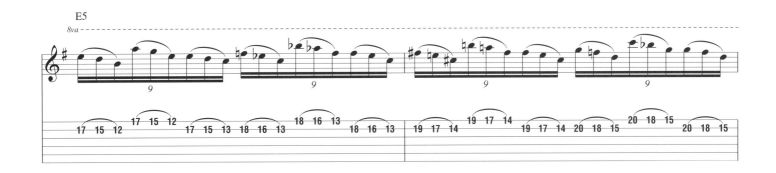

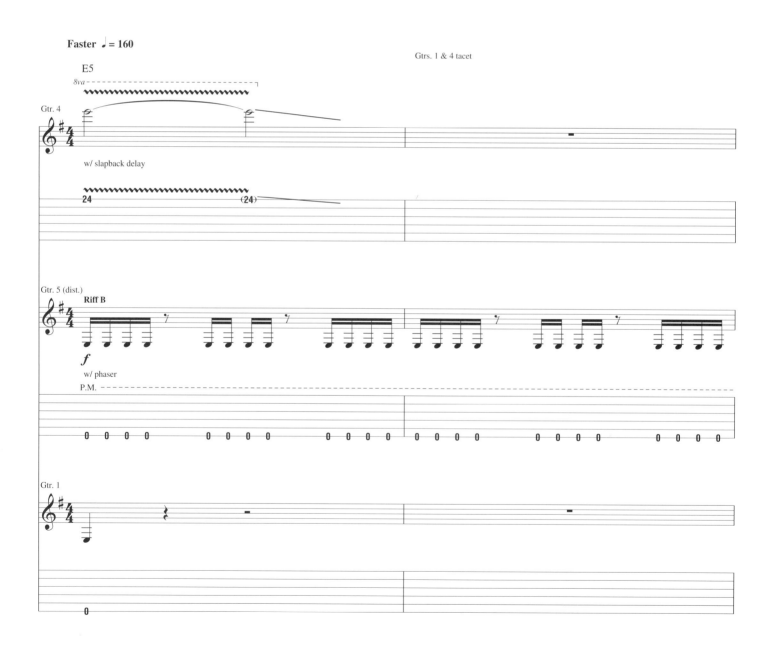

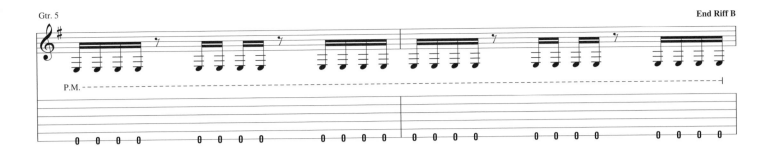

Gtr. 5: w/ Riff B

1. His

Verse

E5

wick - ed high - ness, born _____ from dis - as - ter

Riff C

Gtrs. 1 & 5

f

phaser off

P.M. -

to dom - i - nate _____ and kill. _____

P.M. -

glis - ten - ing ___ mur - der ma - chine, ___ false maj - es - ty ___ stand - ing

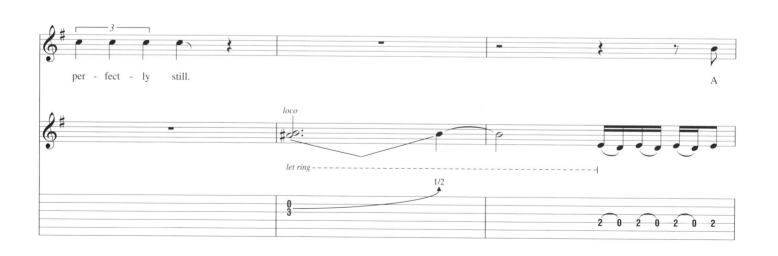

per - fect - ly still.

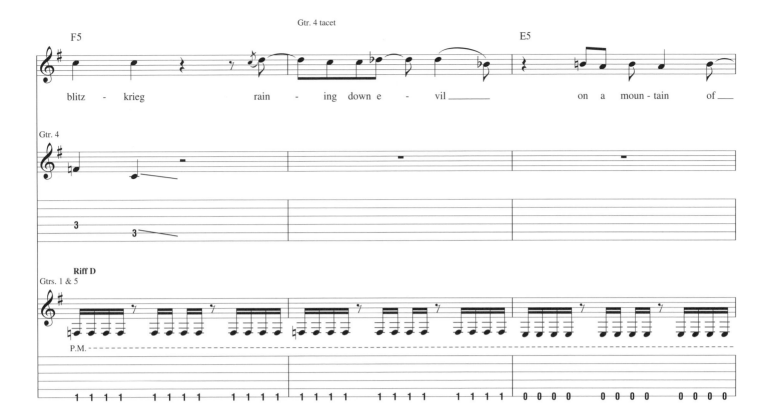

blitz - krieg rain - ing down e - vil _____ on a moun - tain of _____

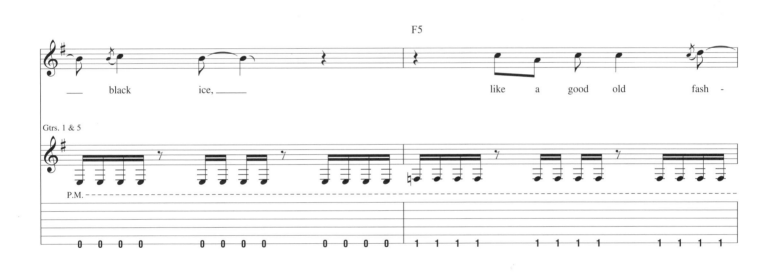

_____ black ice, _____ like a good old fash -

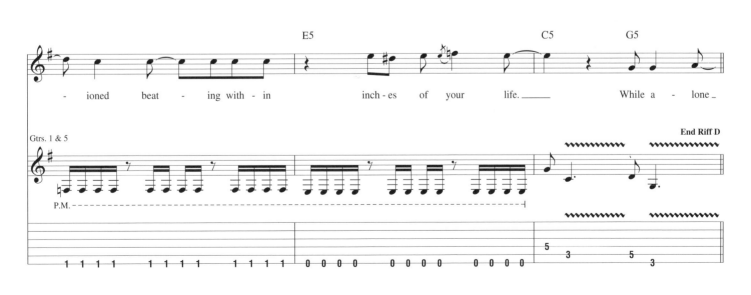

- ioned beat - ing with - in inch - es of your life. _____ While a - lone _____

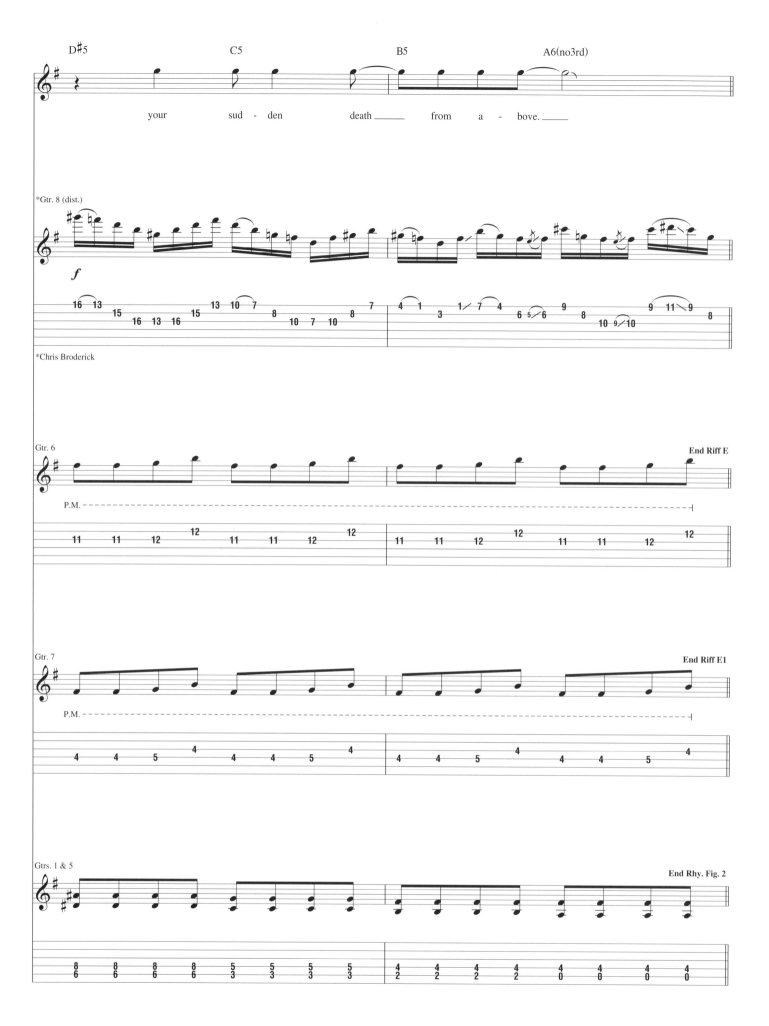

depths of hell.___ Be - queath-ing man,___ noth-ing but de - spair.___

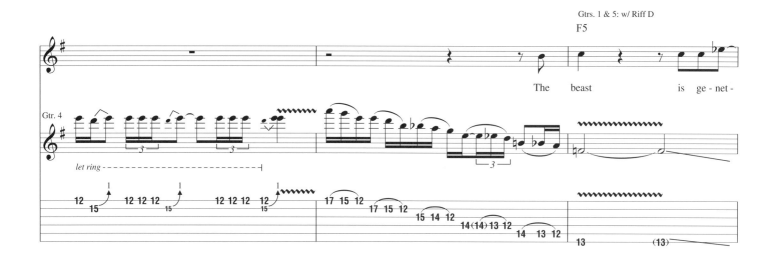

Gtrs. 1 & 5: w/ Riff D

F5

The beast is ge - net -

Gtr. 4

let ring -

Gtr. 4 tacet

E5

- ic - 'ly pro - grammed.   Time to de - stroy,___ time to   go ber - serk.___   To

F5   E5   C5   G5

see   the end ___ of all ___ war,   see   the end __ of the earth. ___

Guitar Solo

E5   F5   E5   D5   D#5   E5   F5   E5   D5   D#5

Gtr. 4

8va -

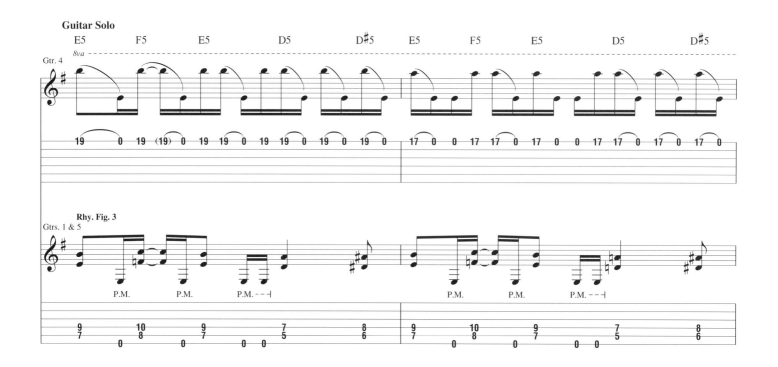

Rhy. Fig. 3

Gtrs. 1 & 5

P.M.   P.M.   P.M. - -   P.M.   P.M.   P.M. - -

Guitar Solo

Gtrs. 1 & 5: w/ Riff F (4 times)

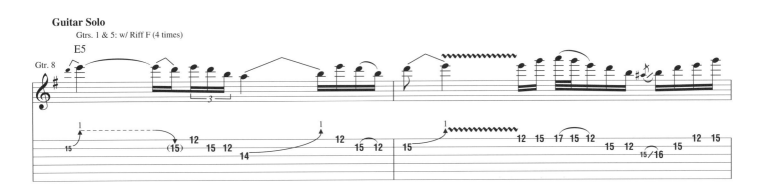

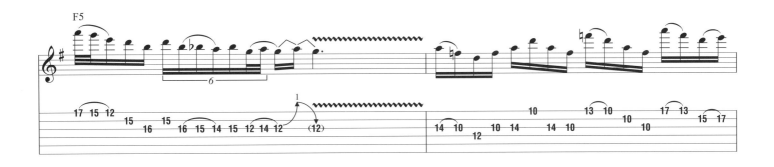

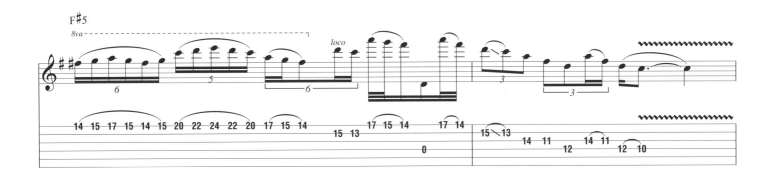

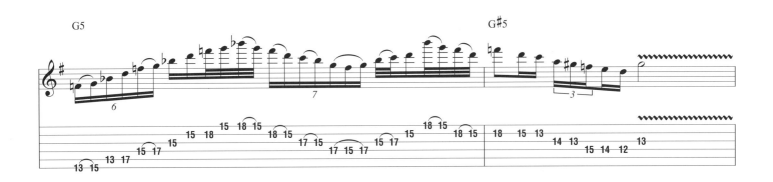

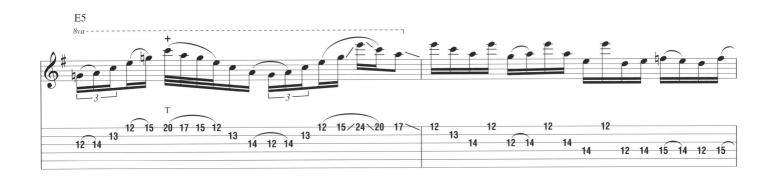

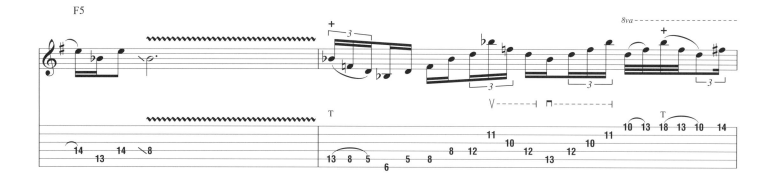

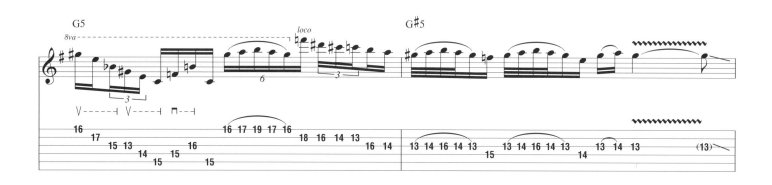

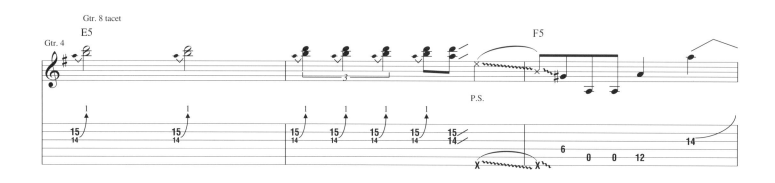

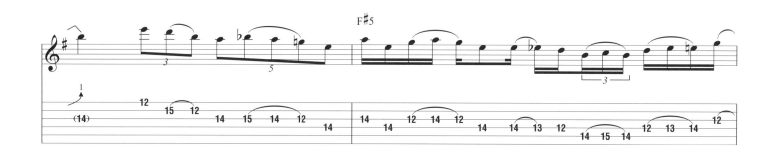

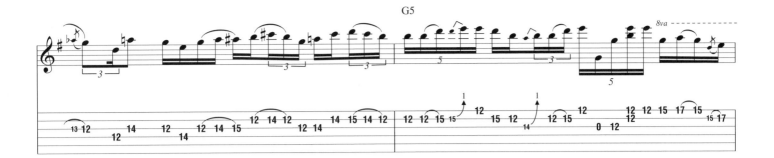

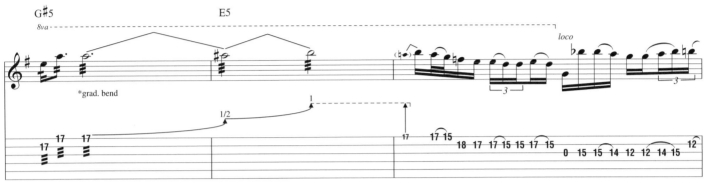

*Pick sixteenth-notes while gradually bending string.

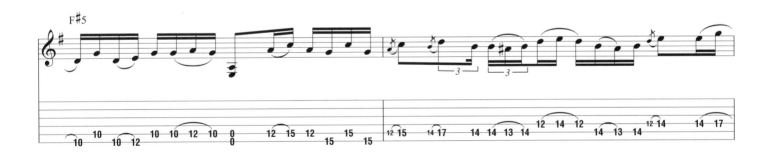

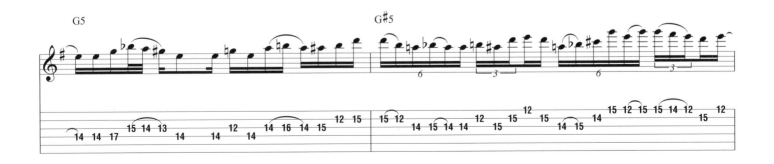

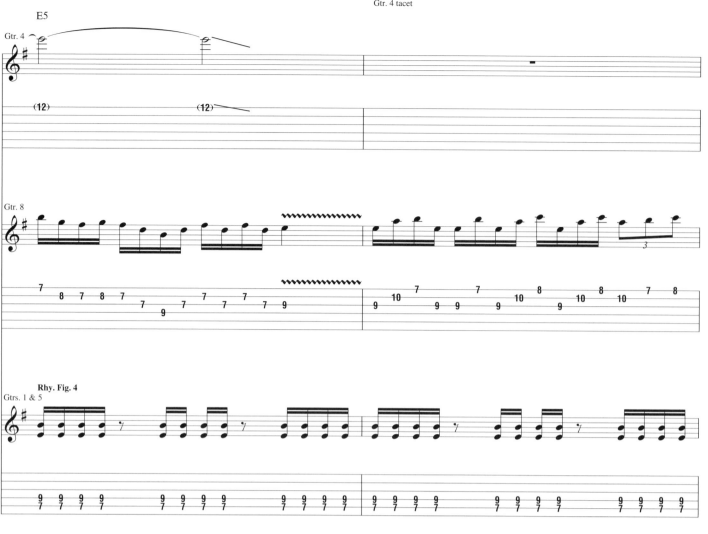

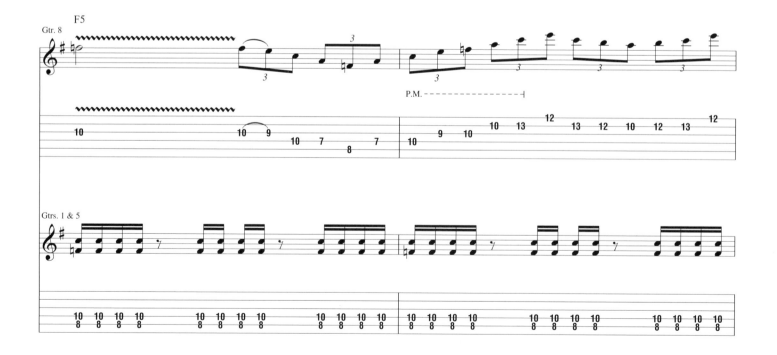

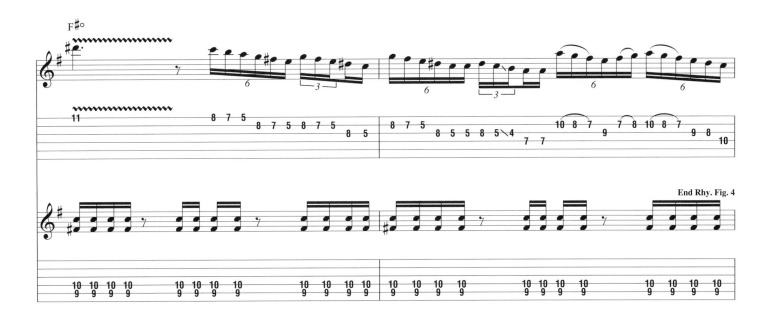

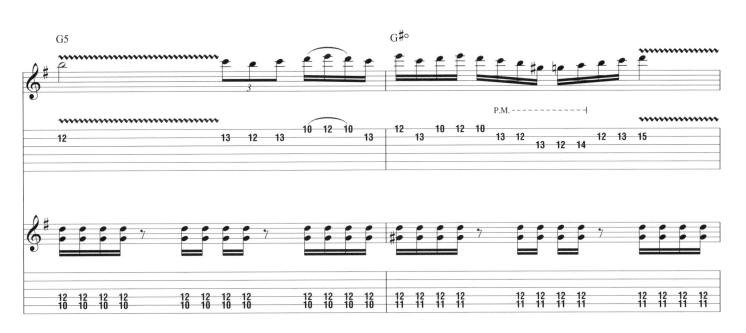

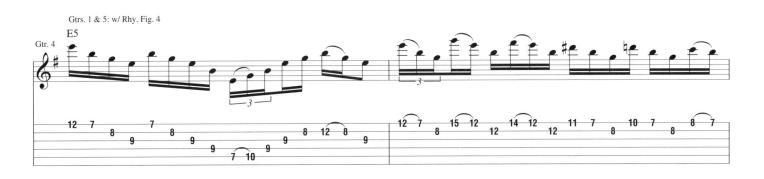

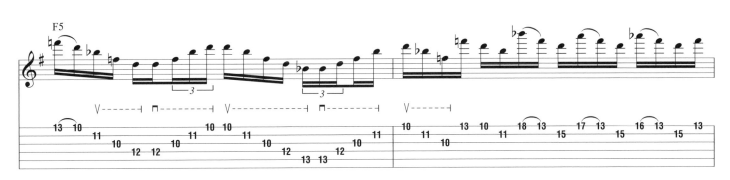

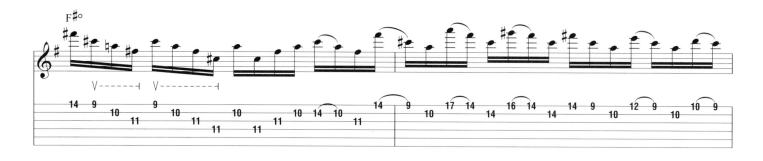

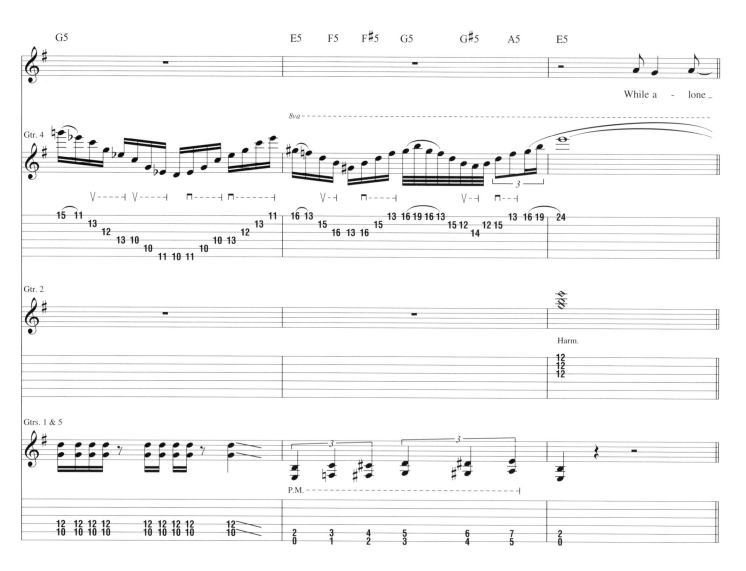

Chorus
Half-time feel
Gtrs. 1 & 5: w/ Rhy. Fig. 2
Gtrs. 6 & 7: w/ Riffs E & E1
Gtr. 2 tacet

Gtr. 4 tacet

— and left a - ban - doned with the sen - tence you've been hand - ed, all your an -

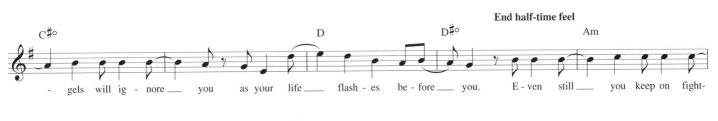

- -gels will ig - nore ___ you   as your   life ___ flash - es   be - fore ___ you.   E - ven   still ___   you   keep on   fight-

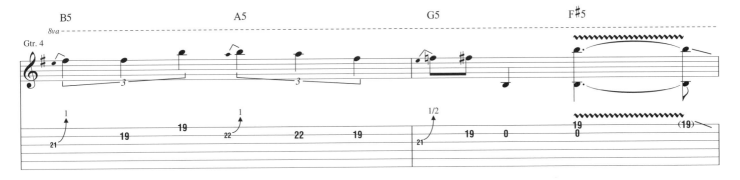

- -ing   through the   thund - der   and   the   light - ning,   and now   heav-en   sends ___ its   love...

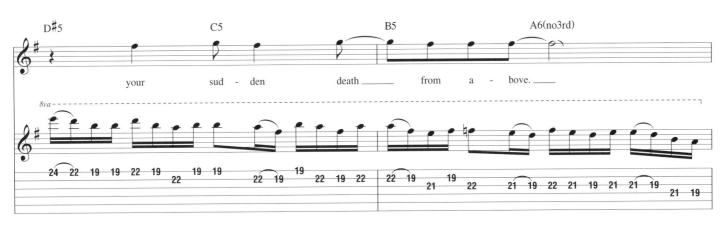

your   sud - den   death ___   from   a - bove. ___

Public Enemy No. 1

Words and Music by Dave Mustaine and John Karkazis

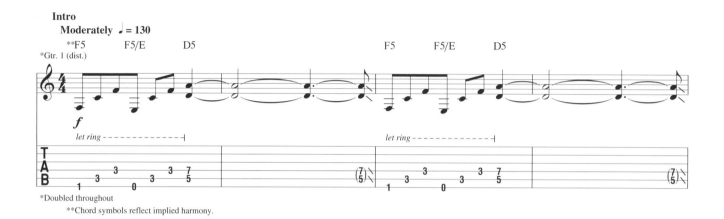

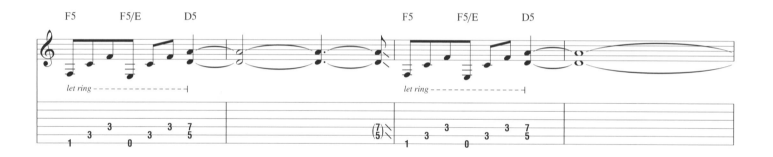

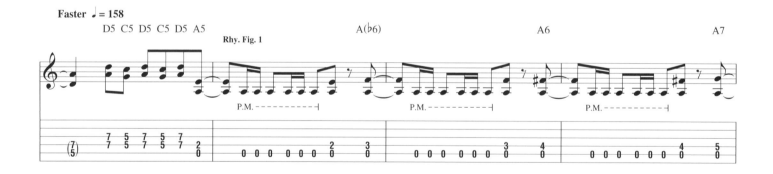

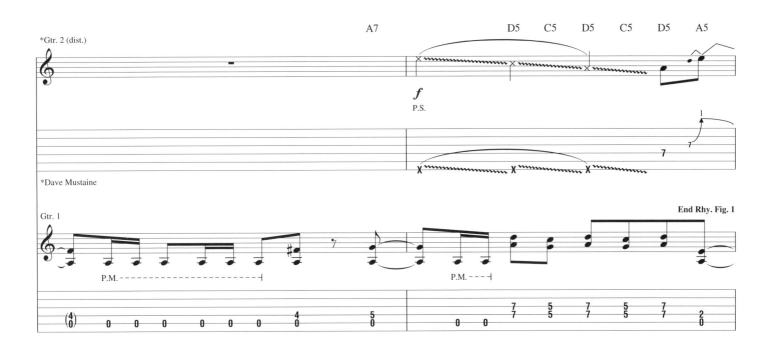

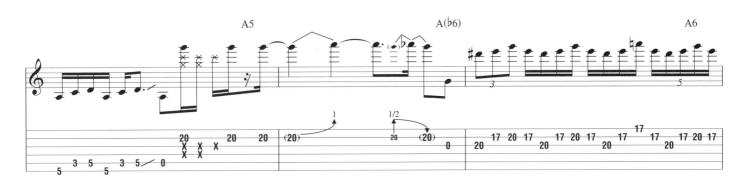

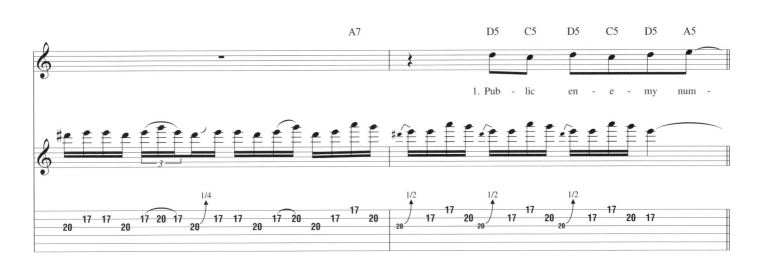

Verse

2nd time, Gtr. 3: w/ Fill 1

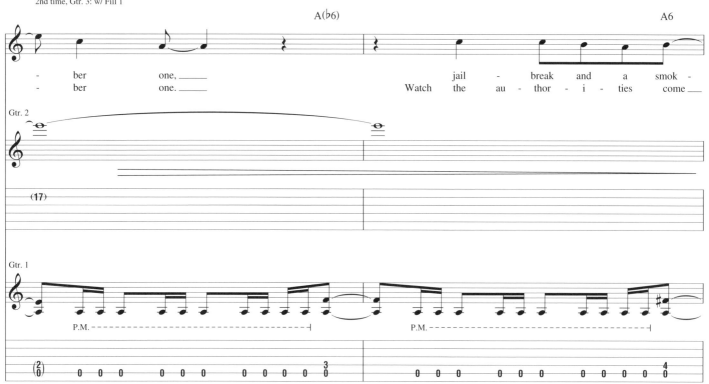

A(♭6)   A6

-ber   one, _____   jail - break   and   a   smok-
-ber   one. _____   Watch   the   au - thor - i - ties   come _____

Gtr. 2

(17)

Gtr. 1

P.M. - ┘   P.M. - ┘

(2/0)

Gtr. 2 tacet

A7   A5   A(♭6)

-ing   gun. _____   You   won't be - lieve   the   things ___   I've   done, ___
___ un - done ___   with   ev - 'ry   stand-off   that ___   I've   won. ___

Gtr. 1

P.M. - - - - - - - - - - - - - ┘   P.M. - - - - - - - - - - - - - ┘   P.M. - - - - - - - - - - - - - ┘

(4/0)

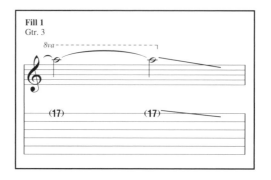

Fill 1
Gtr. 3

8va - - - - - - - - - - - - ┐

(17)   (17)

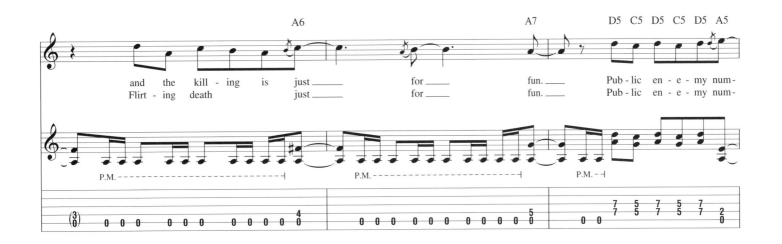

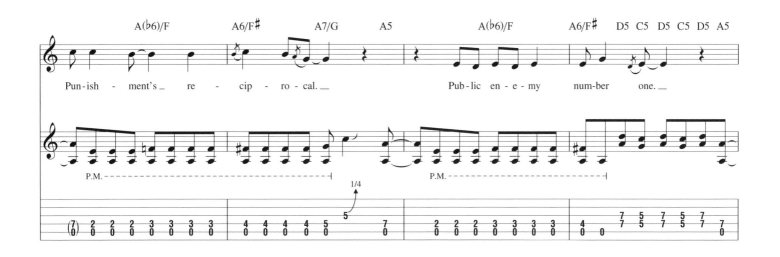

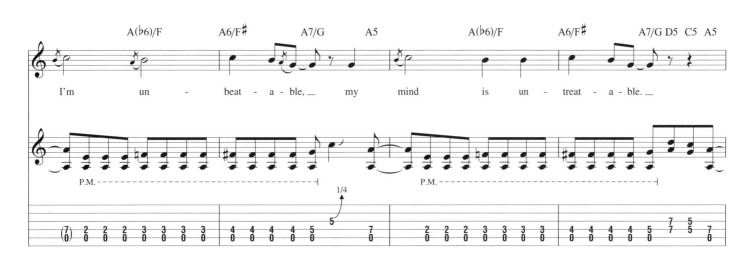

Guitar Solo

Gtr. 1: w/ Rhy. Fig. 1

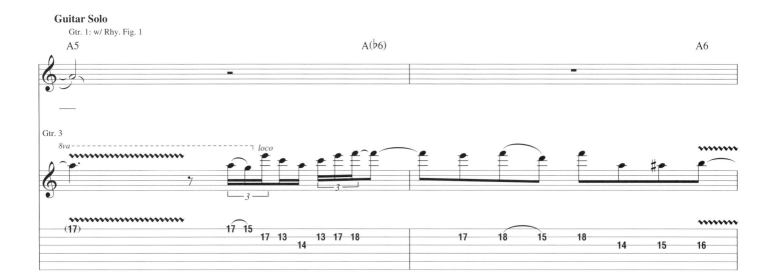

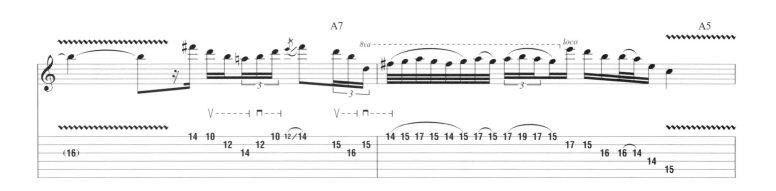

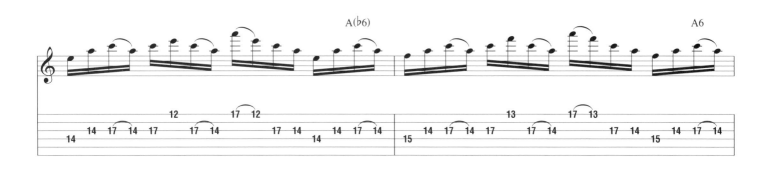

D.S. al Coda 1

2. Pub - lic en - e - my num -

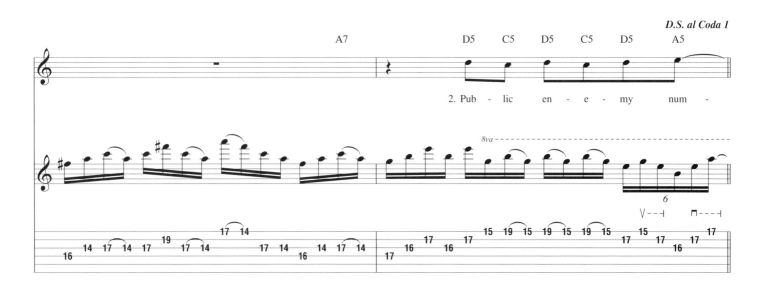

⊕ Coda 1

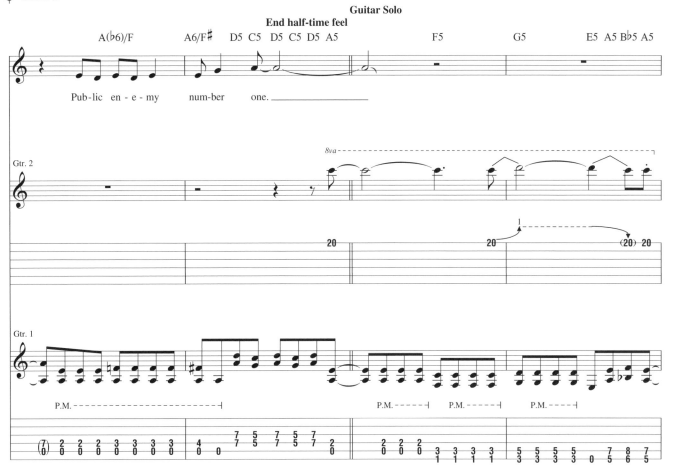

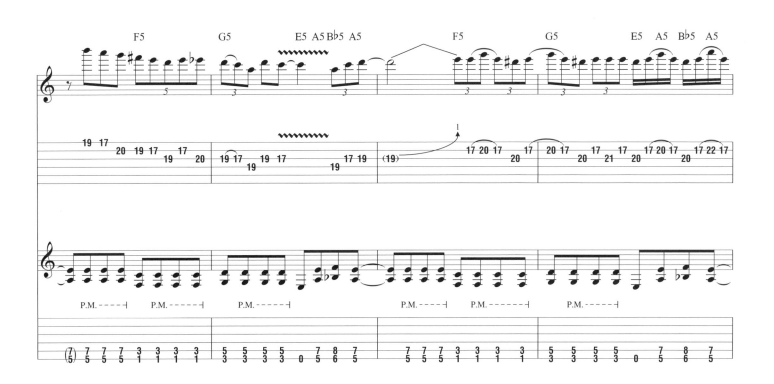

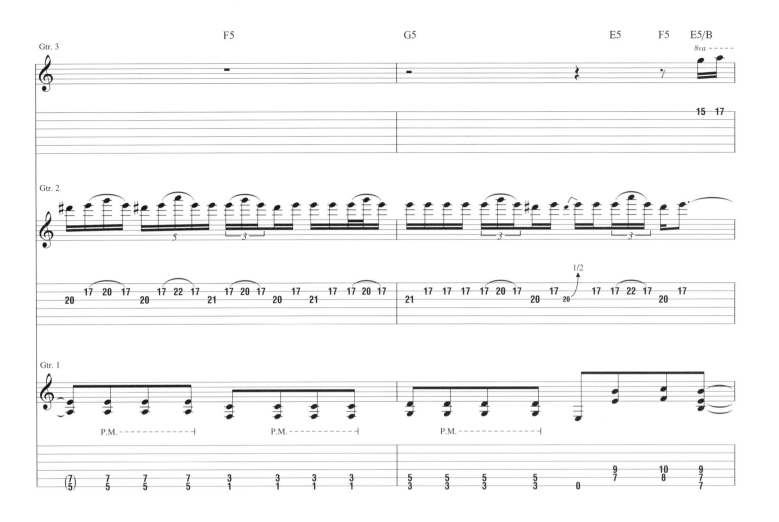

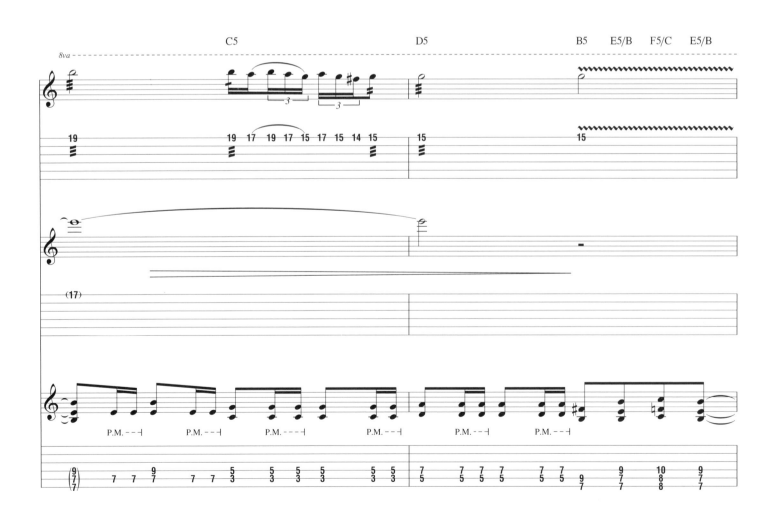

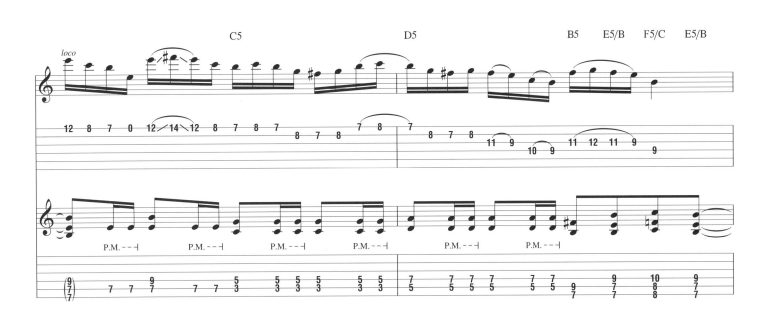

Bridge

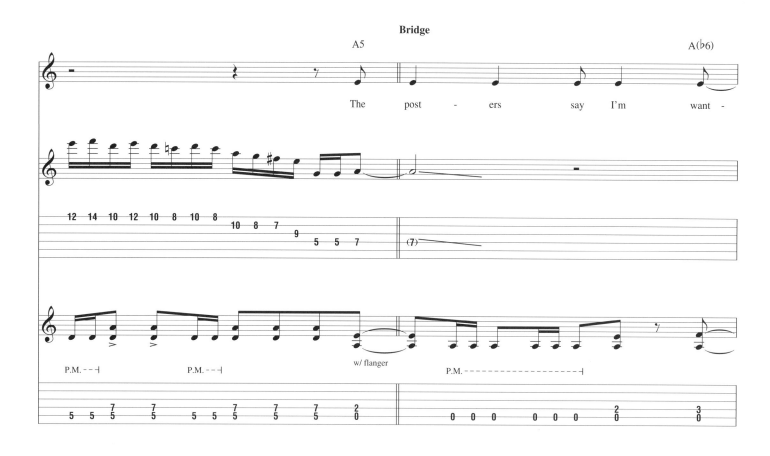

The post - ers say I'm want -

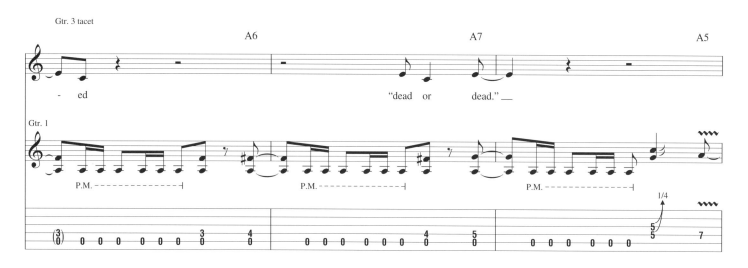

- ed "dead or dead." ―

An - y - one ― who's tried ― got a bul - let to ― the head. ― I'm ―

D.S.S. al Coda 2

34

⊕ Coda 2

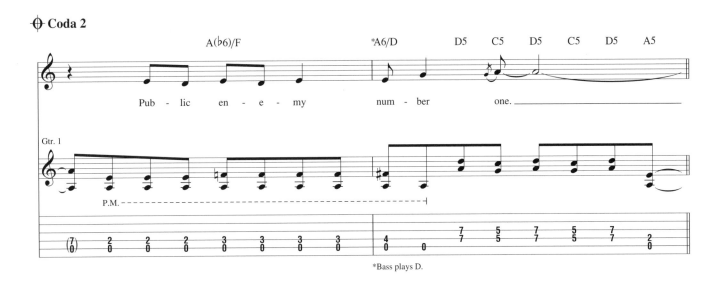

*Bass plays D.

Outro

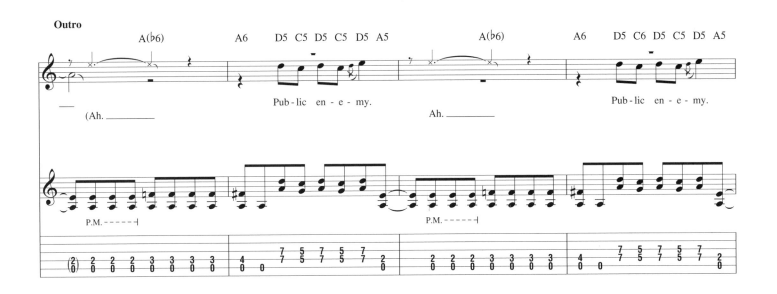

Whose Life (Is It Anyways?)

Words and Music by Dave Mustaine

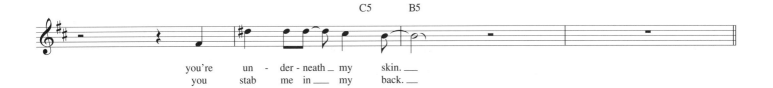

C5   B5

you're   un - der - neath _ my   skin. _
you   stab   me   in _ my   back. _

Pre-Chorus

*E5

You hate the way _ I   wear _ my   clothes. _ You hate my friends _ and   where _ we   go. _

Gtr. 1   **Riff A**   **End Riff A**

P.M. - - ┤   P.M.   P.M. - - ┤   P.M.

*Chord symbols reflect implied harmony.

B5

_   I   see _ you in the _ shad-ows.

P.M. - - ┤   P.M.   P.M. - - ┤   P.M.

Gtr. 1: w/ Riff A

E5

You think you know _ what's best _ for   me. _ You hate _ ev - 'ry - thing _ you   see _

B5   A#5   A5   F#5   F5 E5 D5

_ in me. _   Have you looked _ in a mir - ror?

Gtr. 1

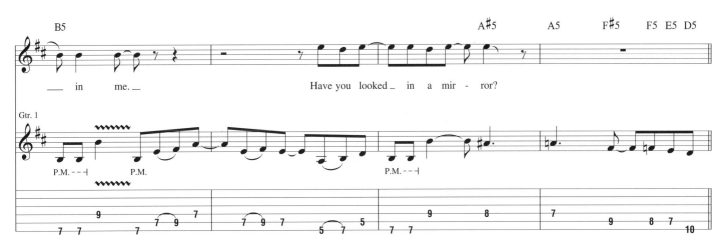

P.M. - - ┤   P.M.   P.M. - - ┤

Gtr. 1: w/ Rhy. Fig. 3

B5   F#5   A5   E5   D5 E5 D5   B5   C5   D5 C5

so much   more — than the price —   I ain't gon-na   pay. _____

Interlude

Gtr. 1: w/ Rhy. Fig. 1

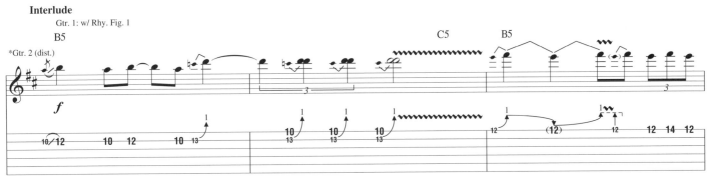

B5   C5   B5

*Gtr. 2 (dist.)

*Chris Broderick

Gtr. 1: w/ Rhy. Fig. 2

D.S. al Coda 1

C5   B5   N.C.

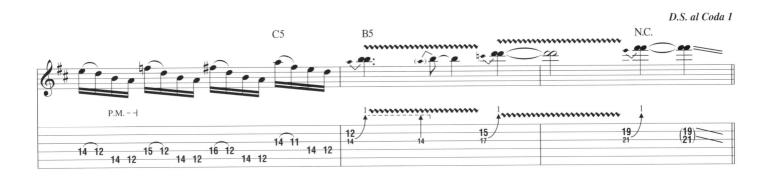

P.M.

⊕ **Coda 1**

Guitar Solo

Gtr. 1: w/ Rhy. Fig. 1 (1 3/4 times)

B5   C5

Gtr. 2

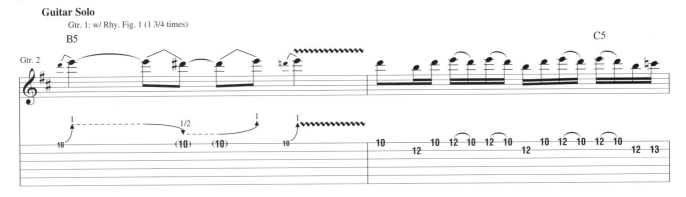

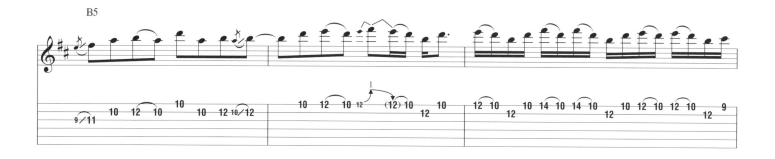

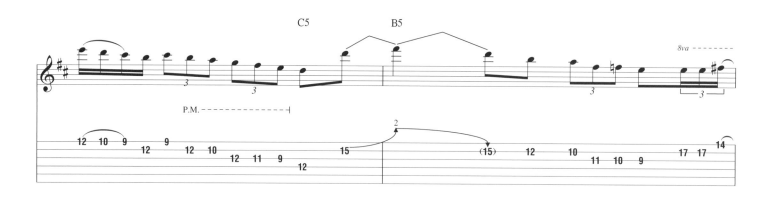

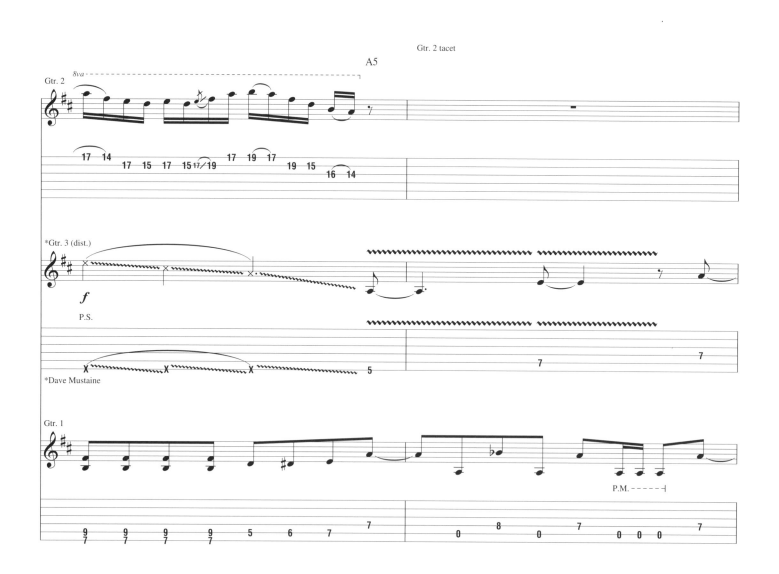

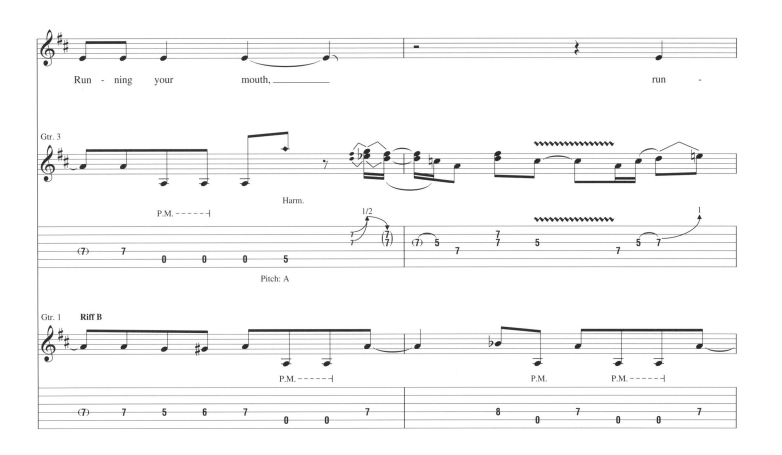

Run - ning   your   mouth, _____   run -

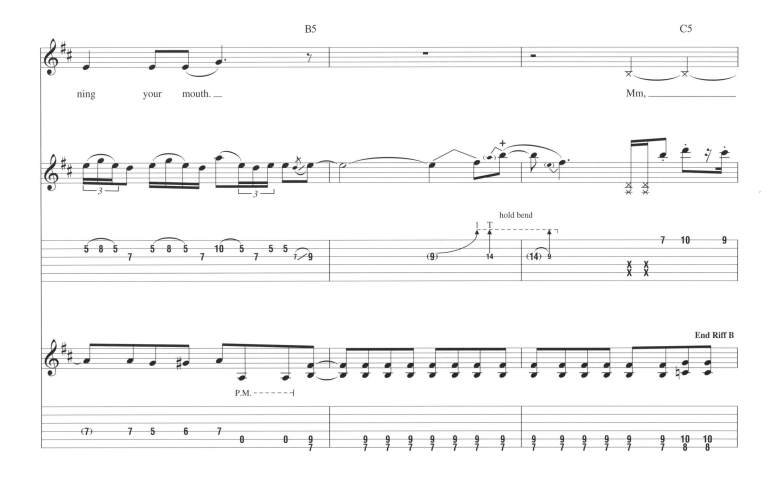

ning   your   mouth. __   Mm, _____

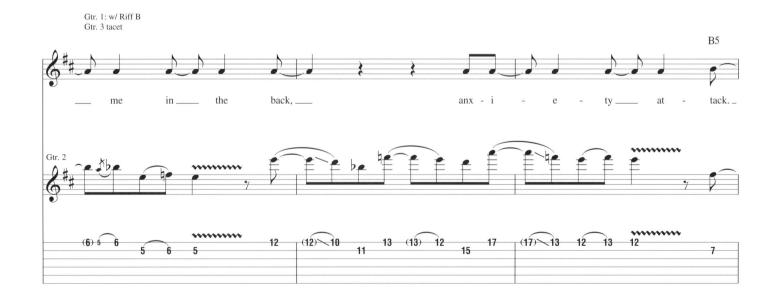

D.S.S. al Coda 2

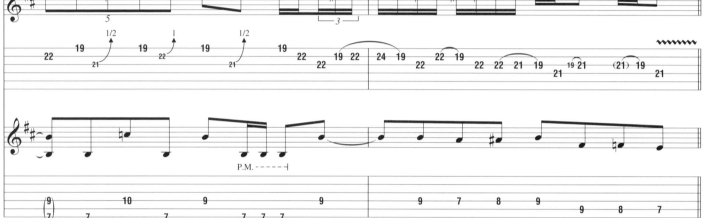

⊕ **Coda 2**

Outro-Chorus

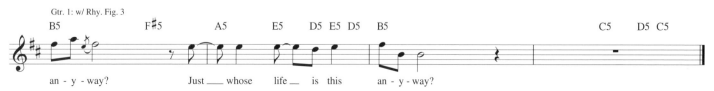

We the People

Words and Music by Dave Mustaine and John Karkazis

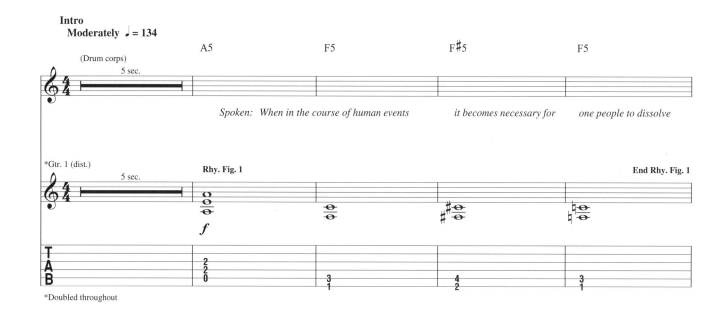

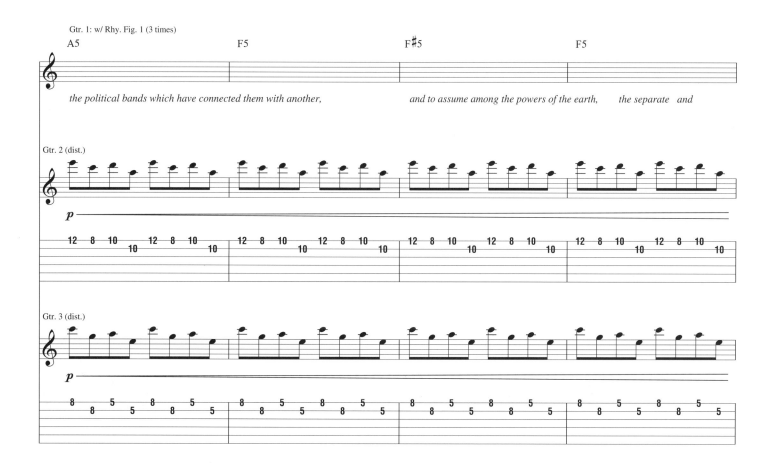

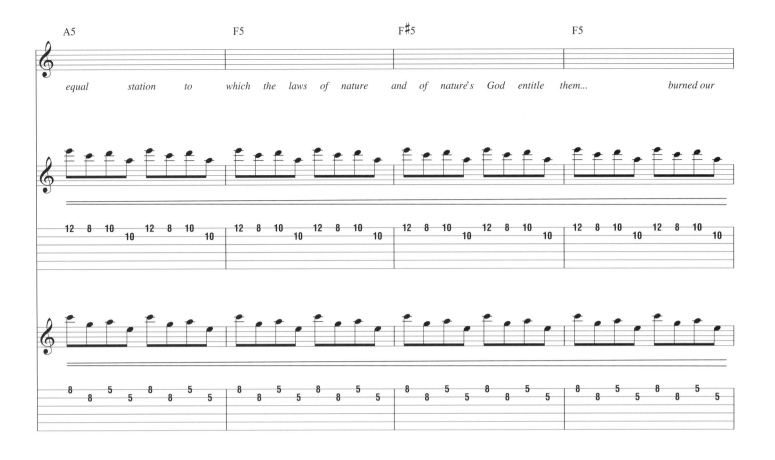

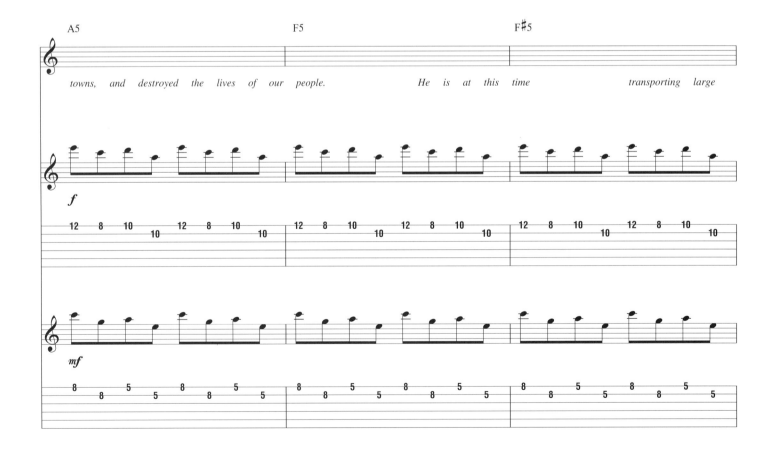

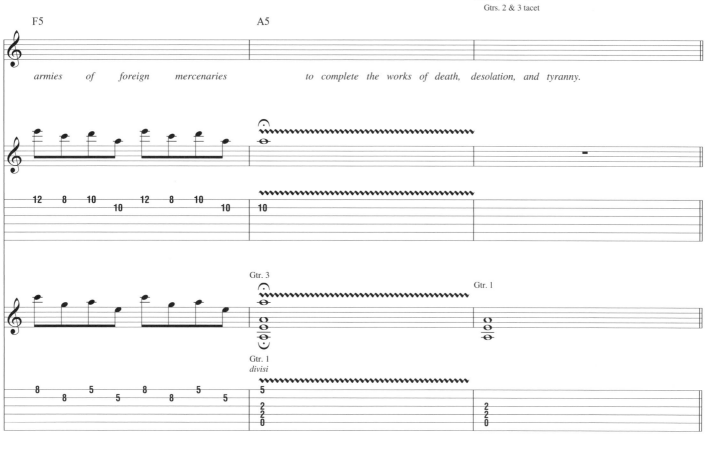

*Chord symbols reflect basic harmony.

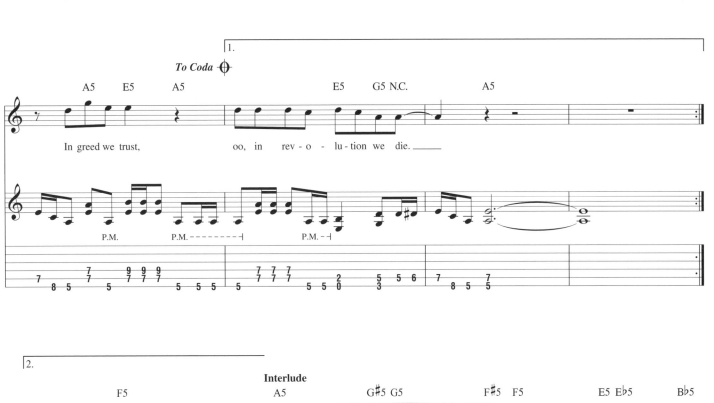

In greed we trust, oo, in rev-o-lu-tion we die.

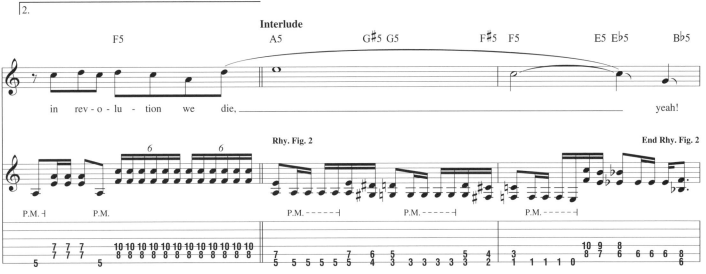

in rev-o-lu-tion we die, _____ yeah!

In rev-o-lu-tion we die! _____

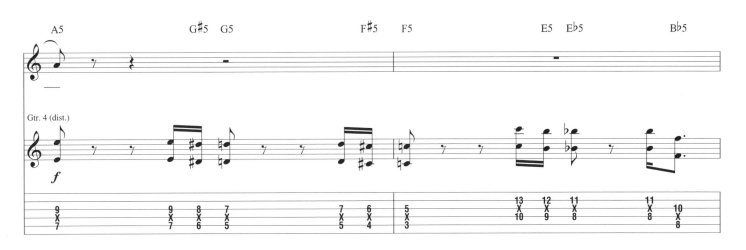

Bridge

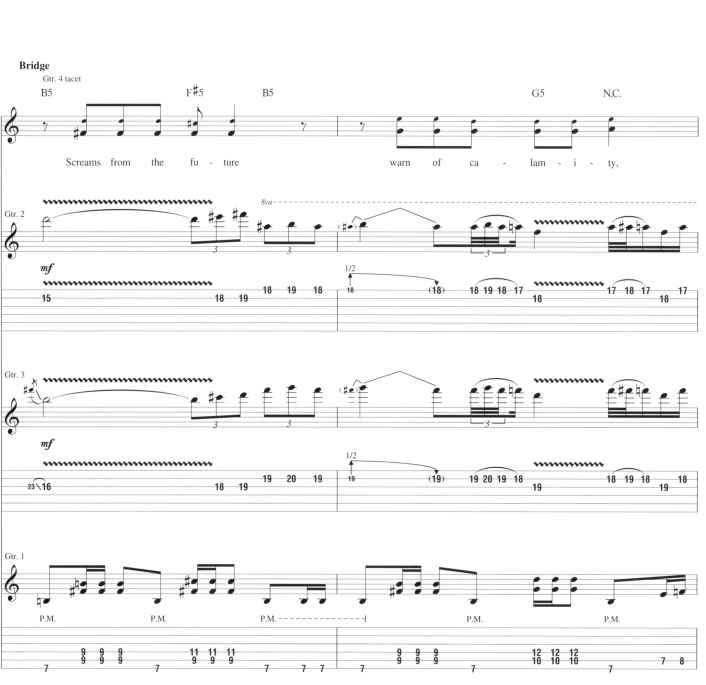

Screams from the fu - ture   warn of ca - lam - i - ty,

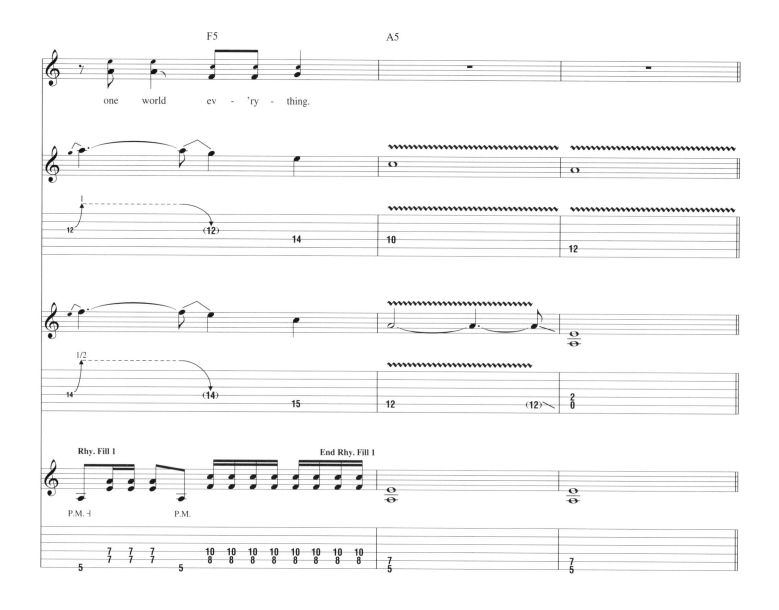

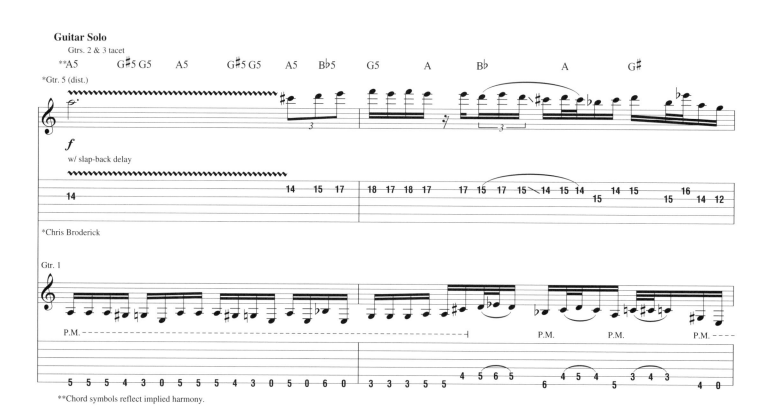

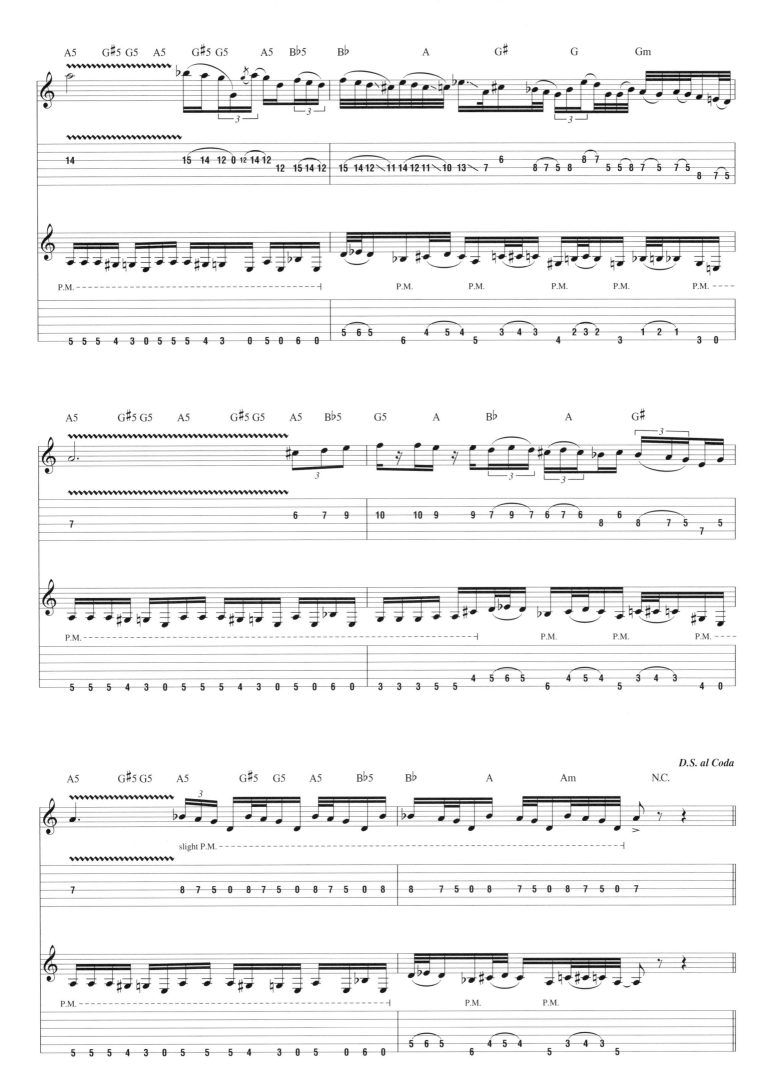

D.S. al Coda

Coda

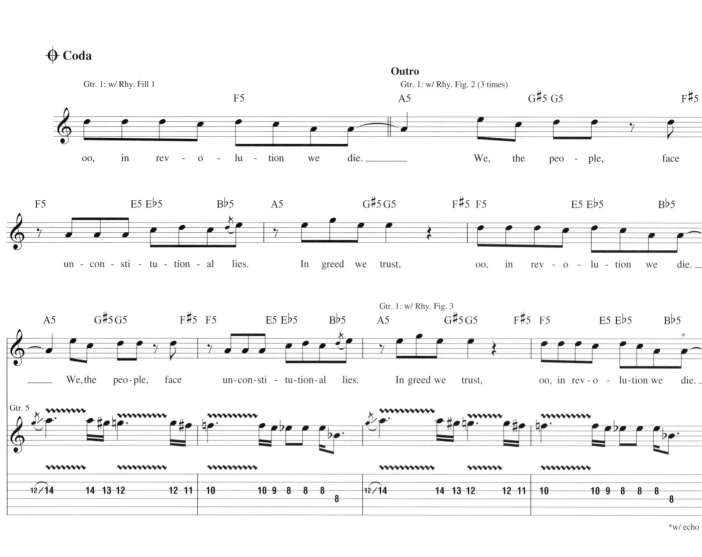

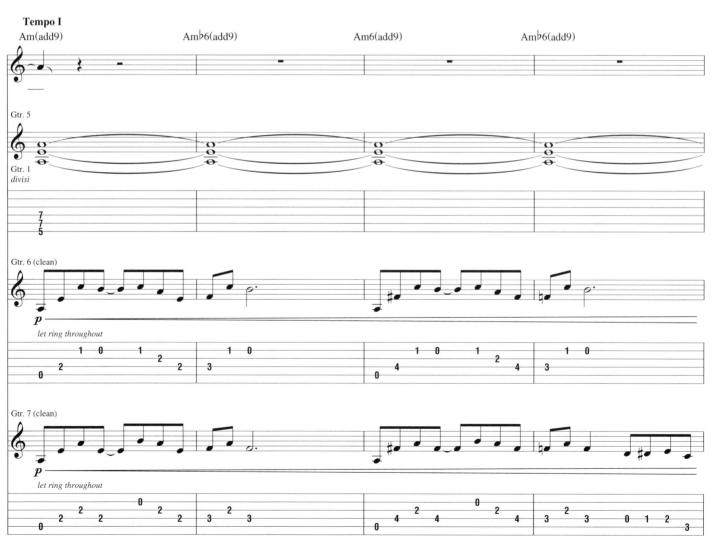

Guns, Drugs, & Money

Words and Music by Dave Mustaine and John Karkazis

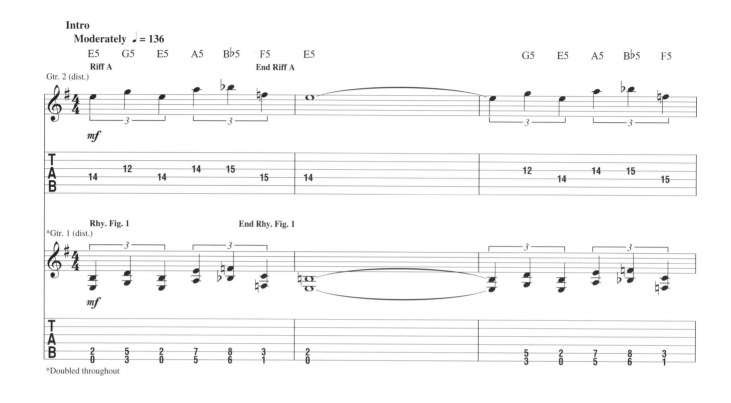

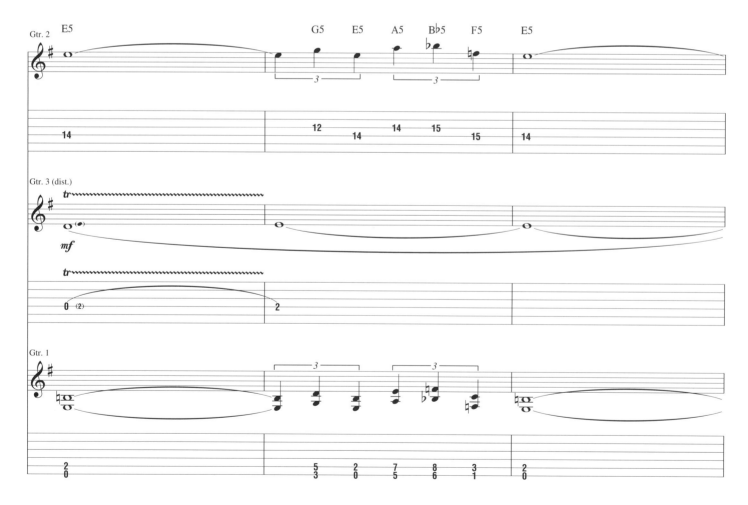

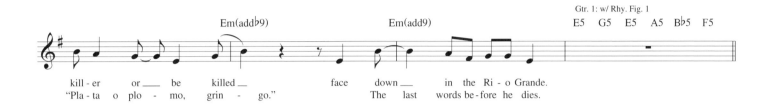

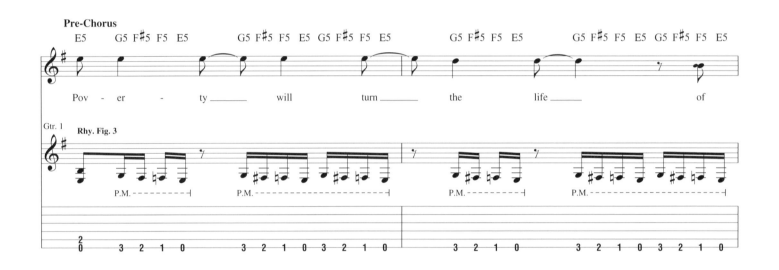

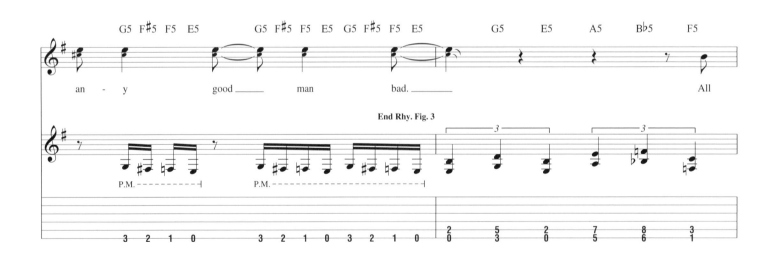

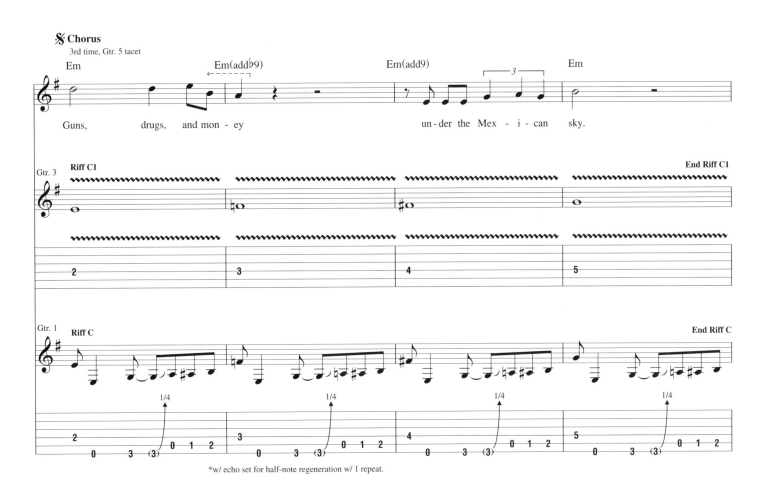

*w/ echo set for half-note regeneration w/ 1 repeat.

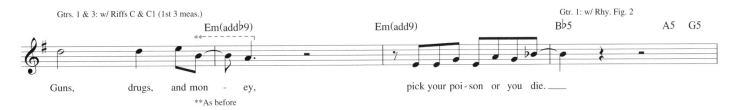

**As before

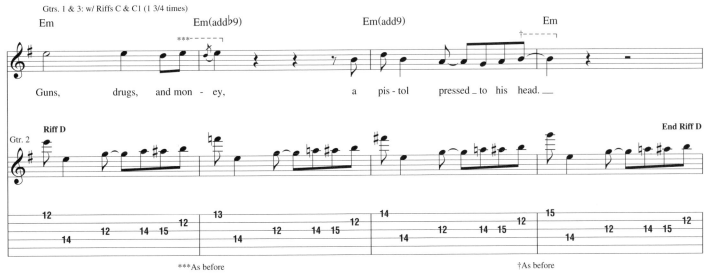

***As before   †As before

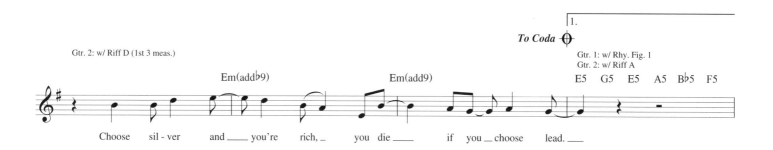

Gtr. 2: w/ Riff D (1st 3 meas.)

Em(add♭9)   Em(add9)

To Coda ⊕

Gtr. 1: w/ Rhy. Fig. 1
Gtr. 2: w/ Riff A

E5 G5 E5 A5 B♭5 F5

Choose sil - ver and ___ you're rich, _ you die ___ if you _ choose lead. ___

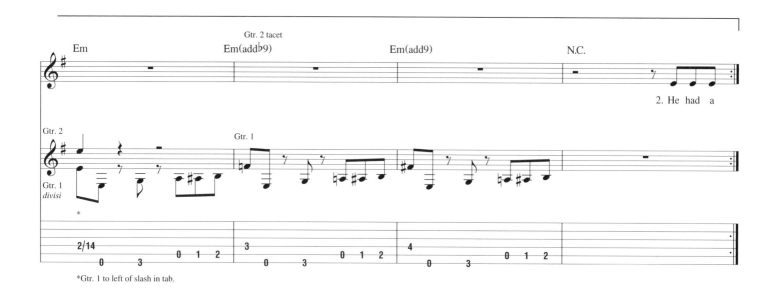

Gtr. 2 tacet

Em   Em(add♭9)   Em(add9)   N.C.

2. He had a

Gtr. 2
Gtr. 1

Gtr. 1
divisi

*

2/14

*Gtr. 1 to left of slash in tab.

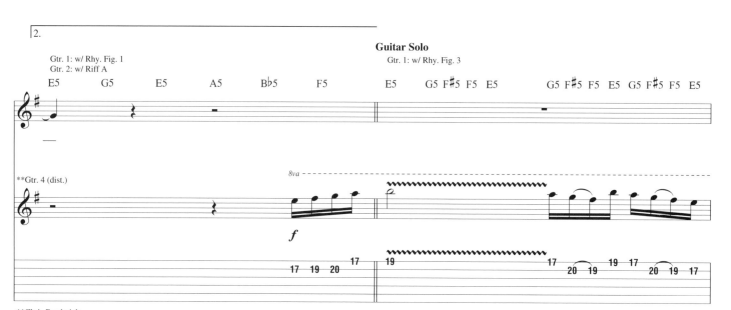

2.

Gtr. 1: w/ Rhy. Fig. 1
Gtr. 2: w/ Riff A

Guitar Solo

Gtr. 1: w/ Rhy. Fig. 3

E5   G5   E5   A5   B♭5   F5   E5   G5 F♯5 F5 E5   G5 F♯5 F5 E5 G5 F♯5 F5 E5

**Gtr. 4 (dist.)

8va

f

**Chris Broderick

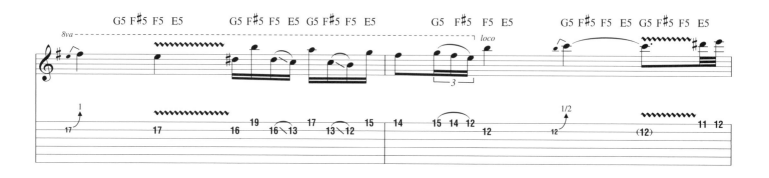

G5 F♯5 F5 E5   G5 F♯5 F5 E5 G5 F♯5 F5 E5   G5 F♯5 F5 E5   G5 F♯5 F5 E5 G5 F♯5 F5 E5

8va

loco

3

1/2

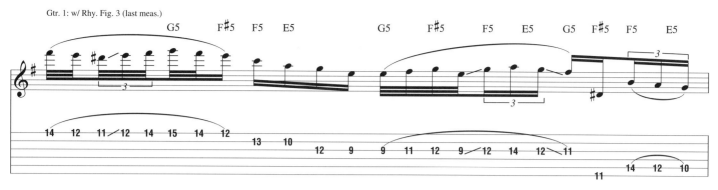

Coda

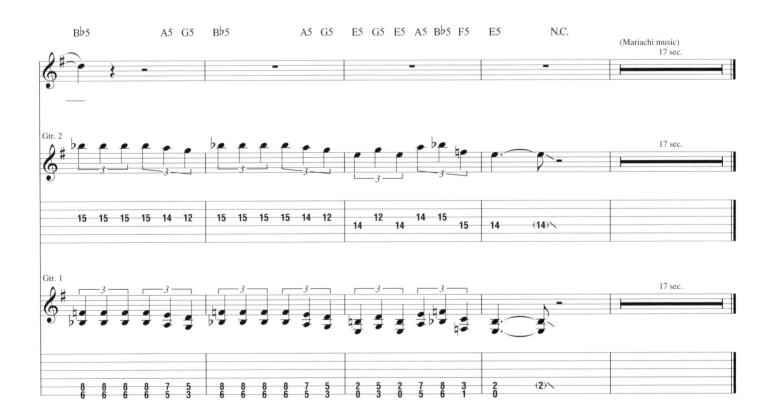

Never Dead

Words and Music by Dave Mustaine

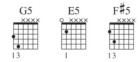

Pitch: G

*Chord symbols reflect implied harmony.

*See top of first page of song for chord diagrams pertaining to rhythm slashes.

(cont. in notation)

Pitch: G

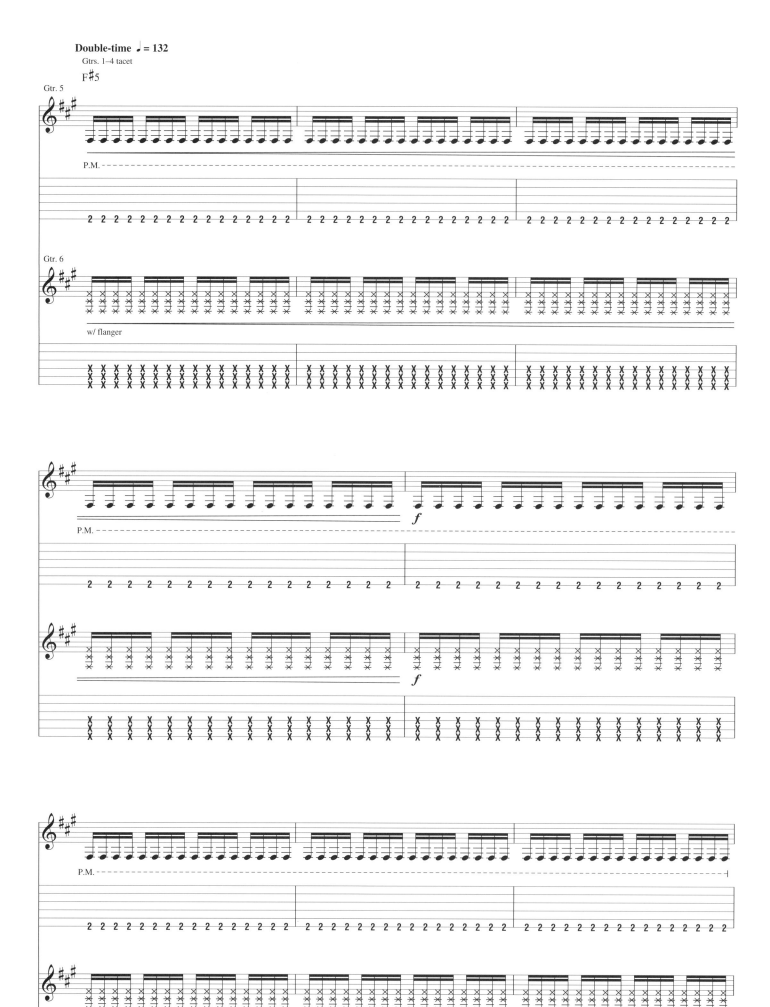

Guitar Solo

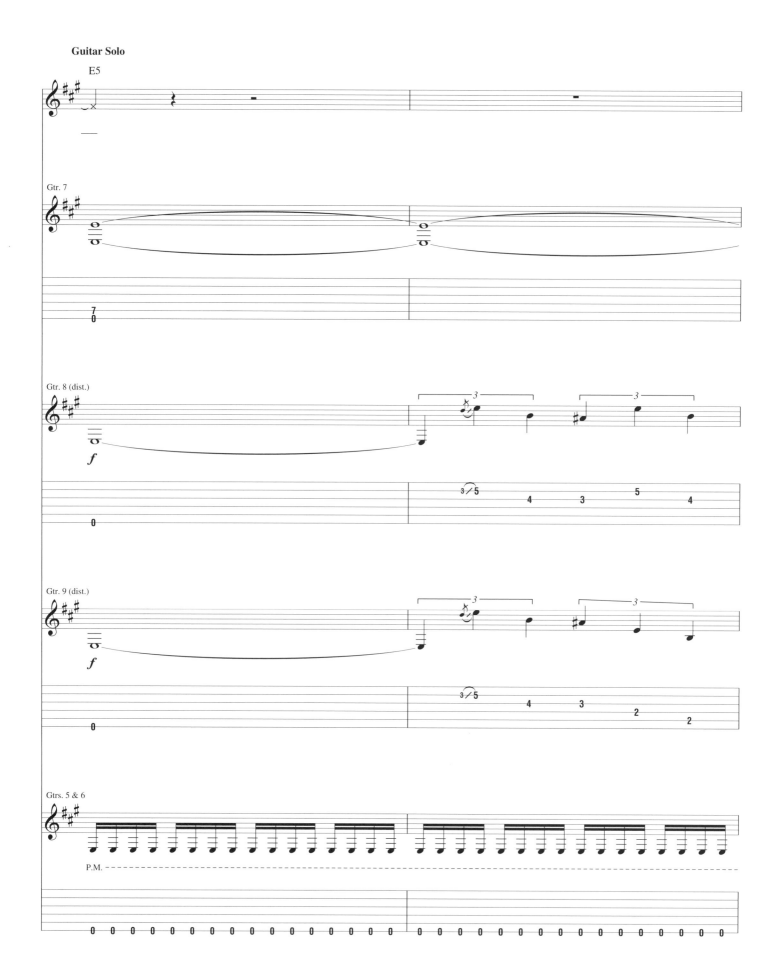

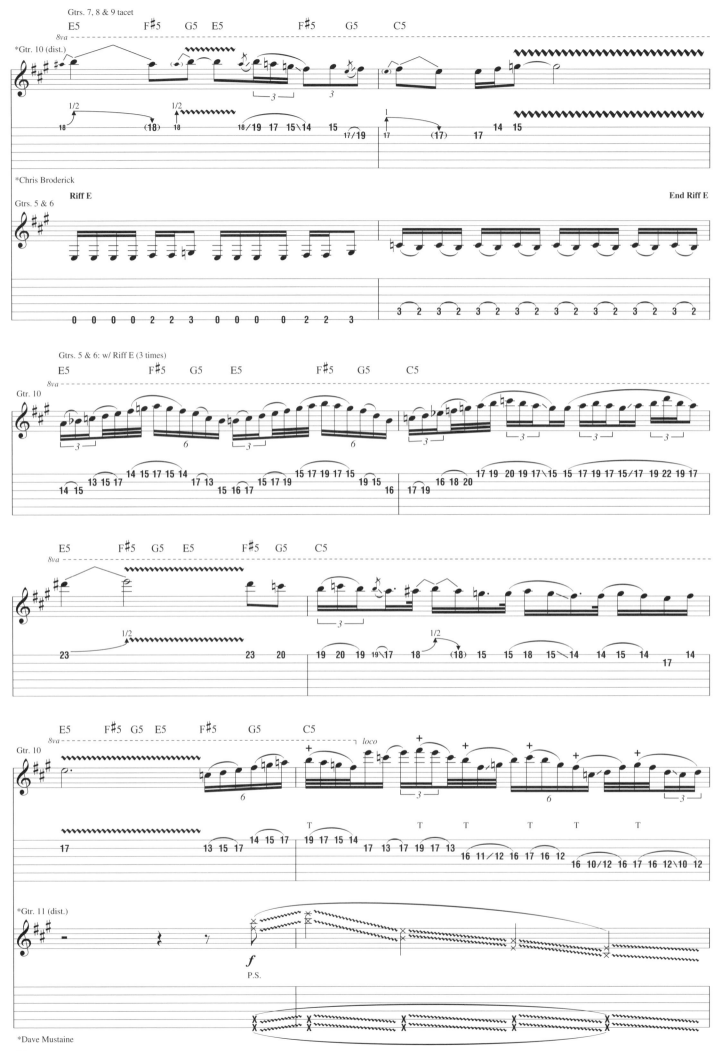

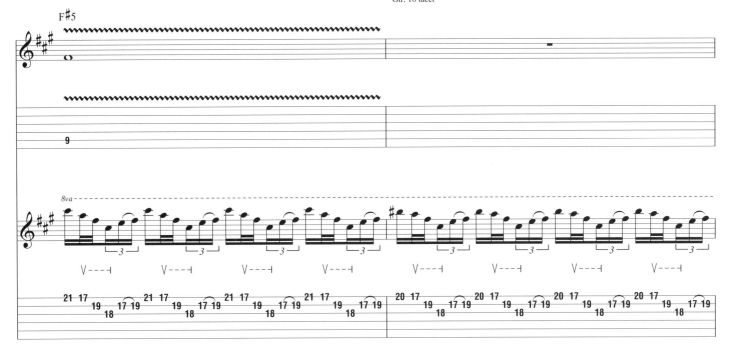

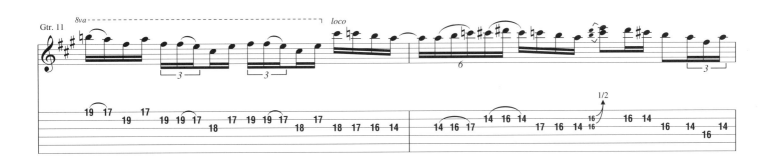

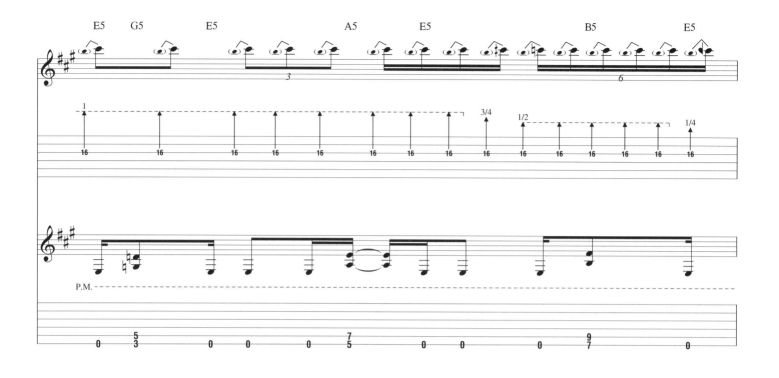

D.S. al Coda

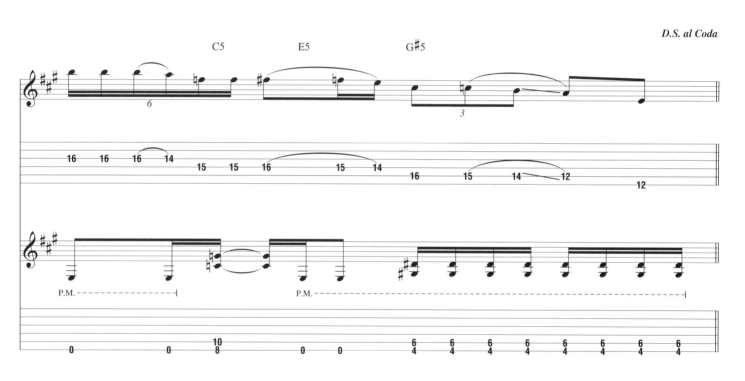

Coda

of the nev - er dead.

New World Order

Words and Music by Dave Mustaine, Marty Friedman, Nick Menza and David Ellefson

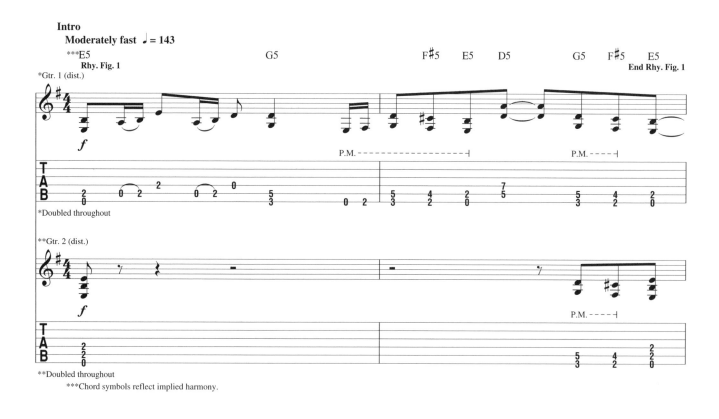

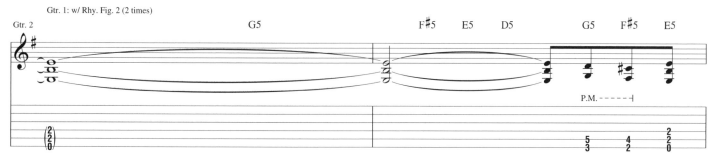

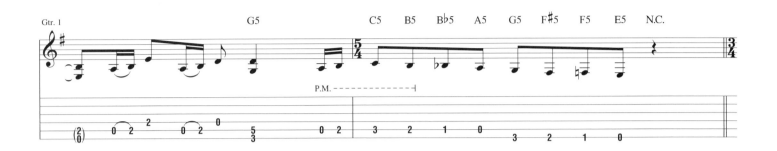

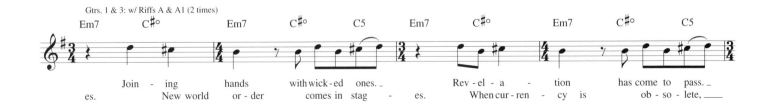

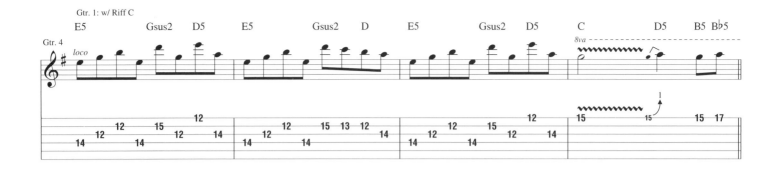

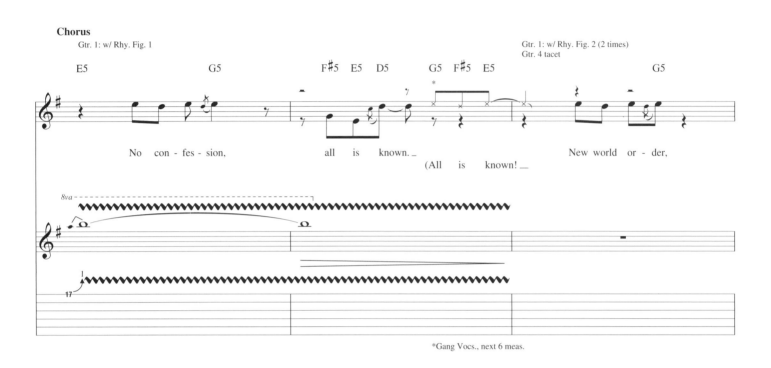

Chorus

*Gang Vocs., next 6 meas.

Guitar Solo

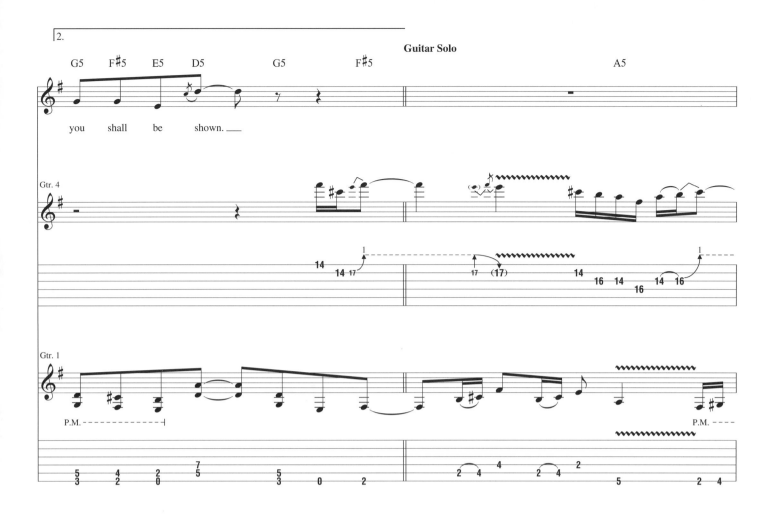

you shall be shown. ___

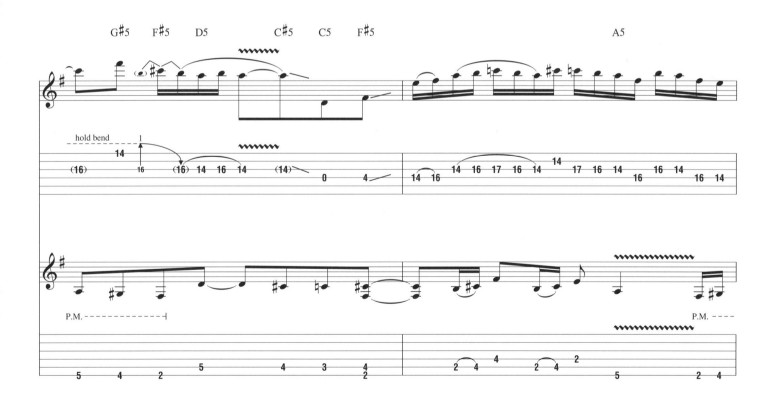

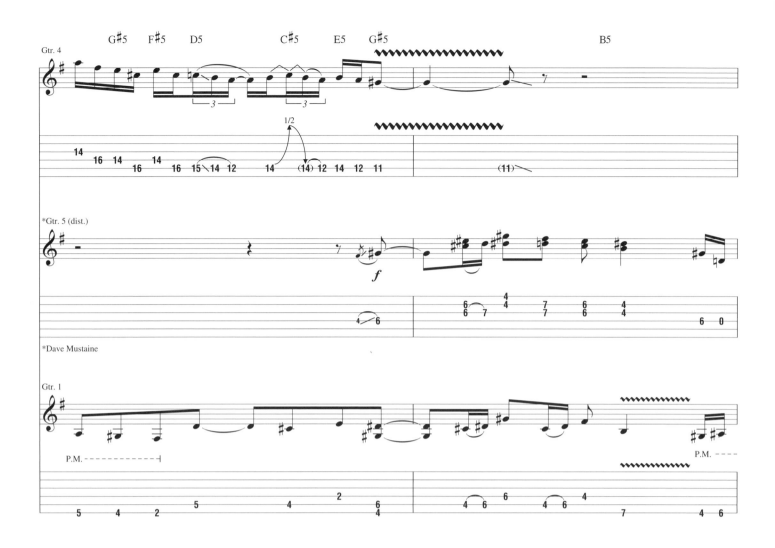

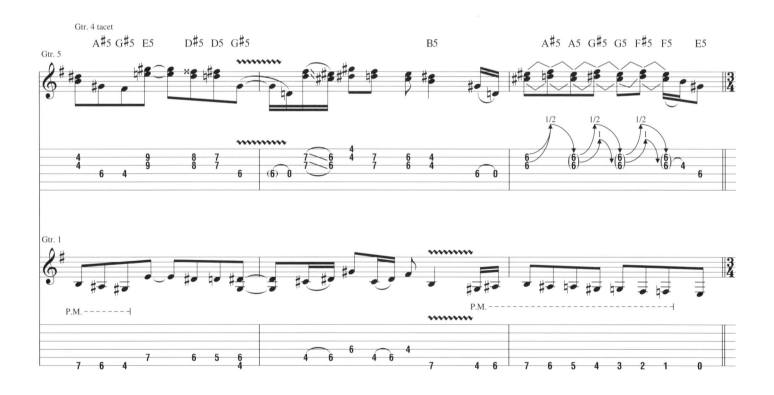

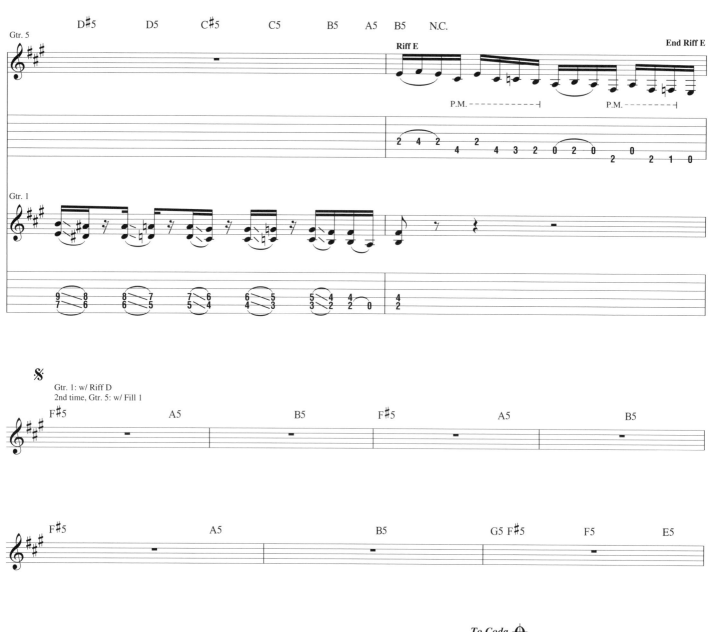

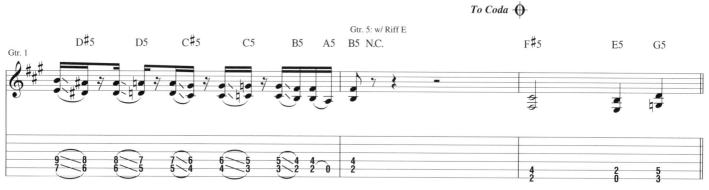

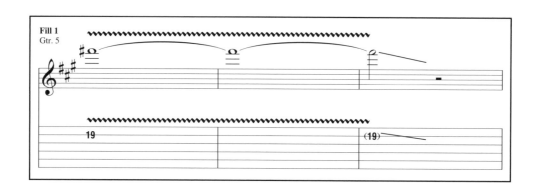

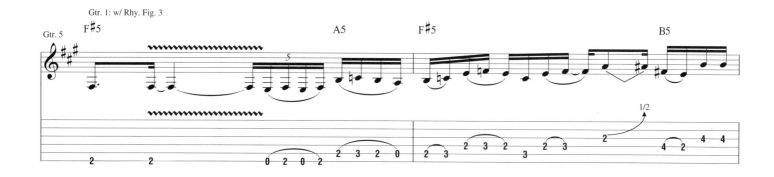

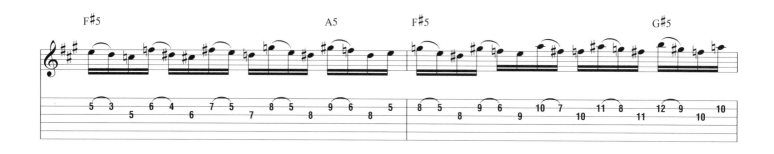

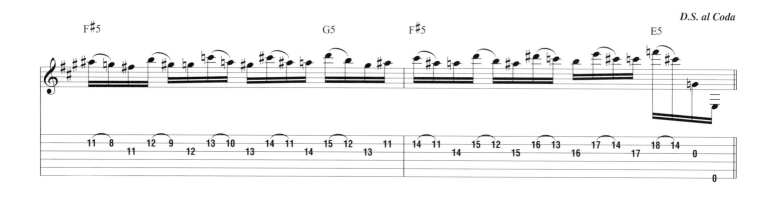

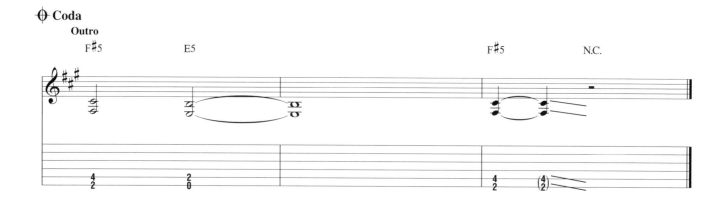

Fast Lane

Words and Music by Dave Mustaine and John Karkazis

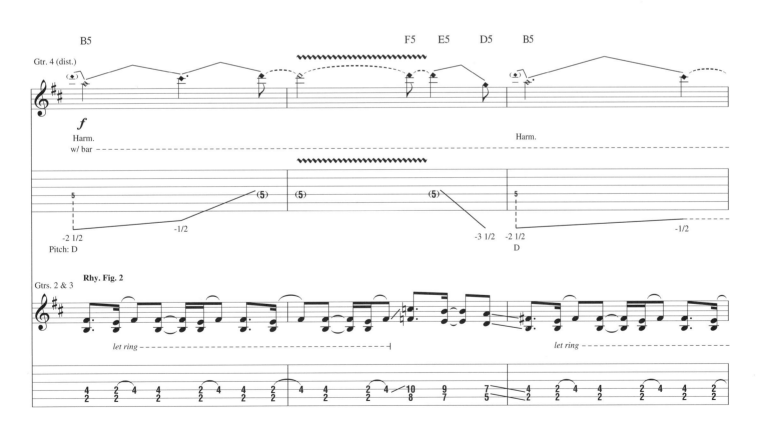

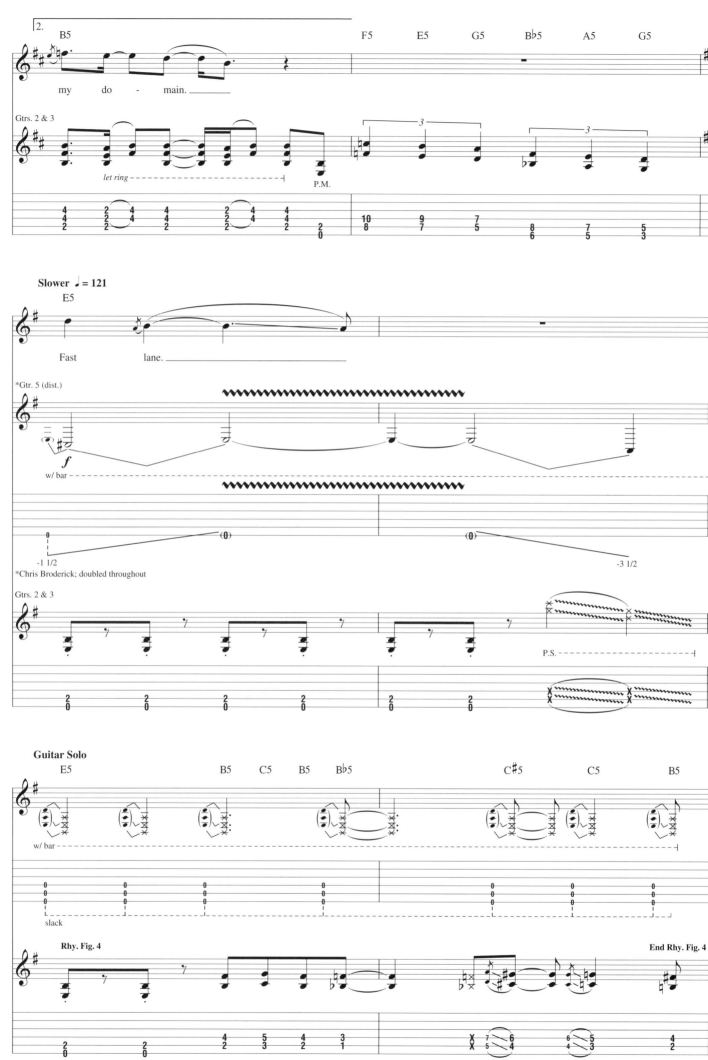

*Lightly touch the strings near the saddles with the pinky side of the pick-hand palm. While executing a trill with the fret-hand, produce random harmonics by gradually sliding the pick-hand along the strings away from, then toward the bridge.

**Gradually lift P.M.

93

**See top of first page of song for chord diagram pertaining to rhythm slashes.

Black Swan

Words and Music by Dave Mustaine

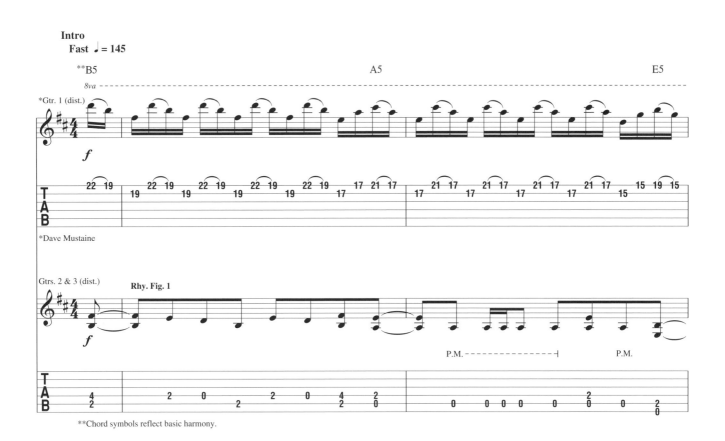

Intro
Fast ♩ = 145

*Dave Mustaine

**Chord symbols reflect basic harmony.

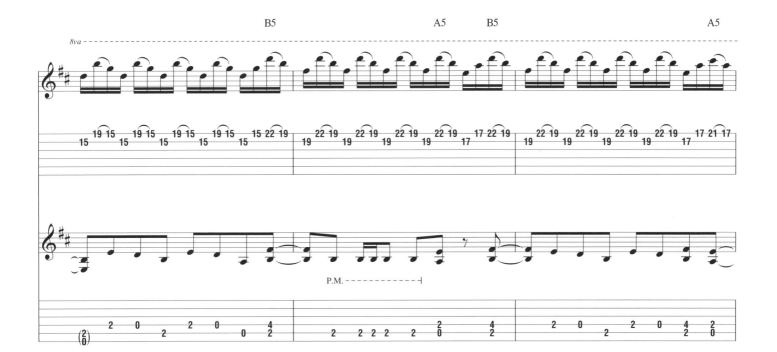

Verse

1. I thought a de - sire ___ worth an - y pleas - ure ___

can nev - er real - ly be ___ a sin in ___ vain. ___

One hun - dred and one ___ shots of ___ op - por - tu - ni - ty,

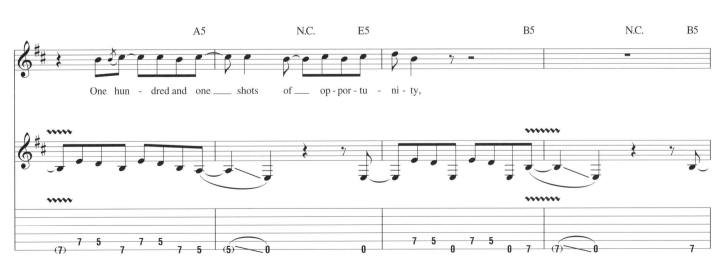

Chorus

Just like a church - yard shad - ow creep - ing af - ter me,

it's on - ly there to ter - ri - fy my mind. A black swan keeps haunt-ing me.

Interlude

Gtr. 2: w/ Riff A (2 times)
Gtr. 3: w/ Riff A (1 1/2 times)

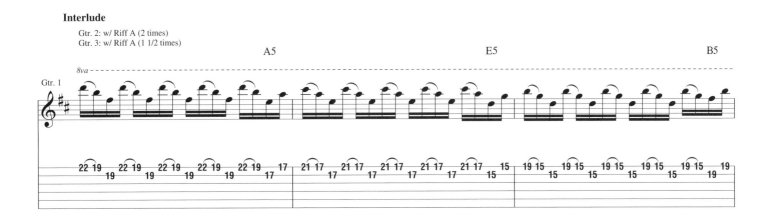

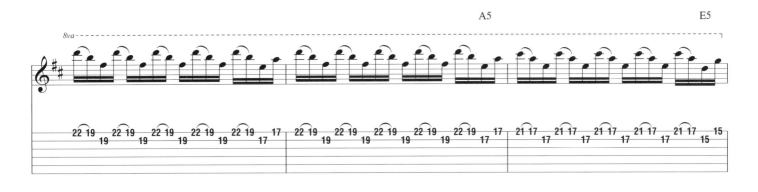

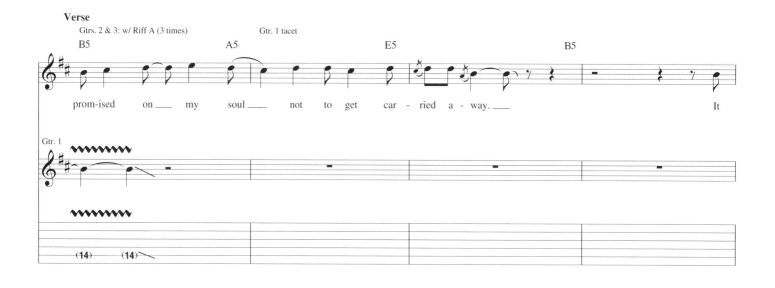

Verse

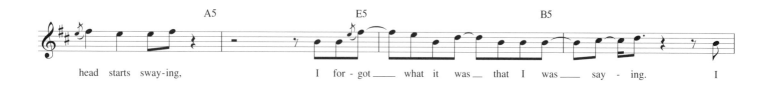

don't know where I am ___ and I'll nev-er, nev-er make it back. ___

Gtrs. 2 & 3

Bridge

Oo, I sealed my fate, ___ and I paid my debt. ___

*Chord symbols reflect harmony implied by Bass (next 6 meas.).

I fell from grace ___ with deep ___ re-gret. ___

Pre-Chorus

Gtrs. 2 & 3: w/ Rhy. Fig. 2

Gtrs. 2 & 3: w/ Rhy. Fig. 3 (1st meas.)

My an-gels left ___ me with sor-rows all my own. ___ And now ___ I'm here ___

with the dev - il all __ my own. __

Gtrs. 2 & 3

Chorus
Gtrs. 2 & 3: w/ Rhy. Fig. 4 (8 times)

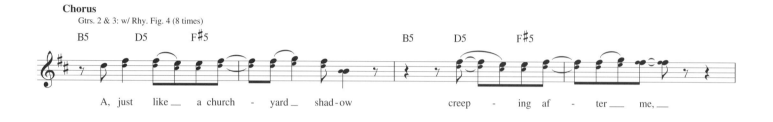

A, just like __ a church - yard __ shad - ow creep - ing af - ter __ me, __

it's on - ly there __ to ter - ri - fy __ my mind. __ A black swan __ keeps haunt-ing me.

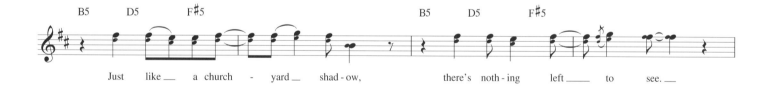

Just like __ a church - yard __ shad - ow, there's noth - ing left __ to see. __

It's on - ly there __ to ter - ri - fy __ my mind. __ A black swan __ keeps haunt-ing me. __

*Gtr. 4 (dist.)

*Chris Broderick

Guitar Solo

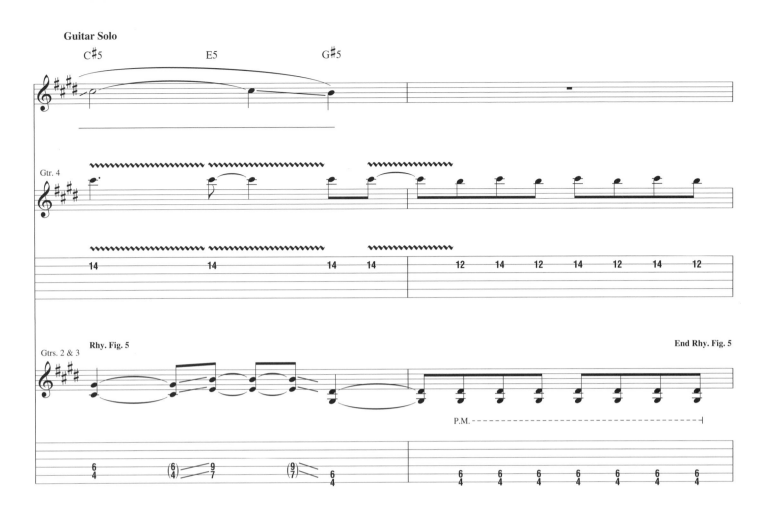

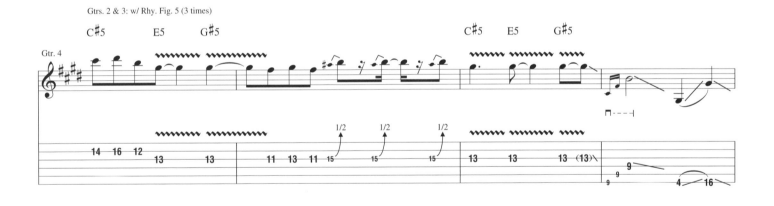

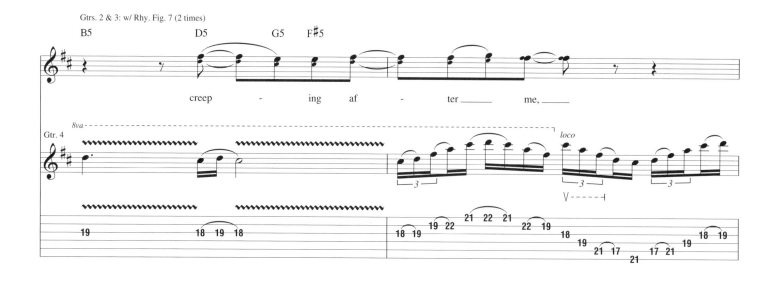

creep - ing af - ter ____ me, ____

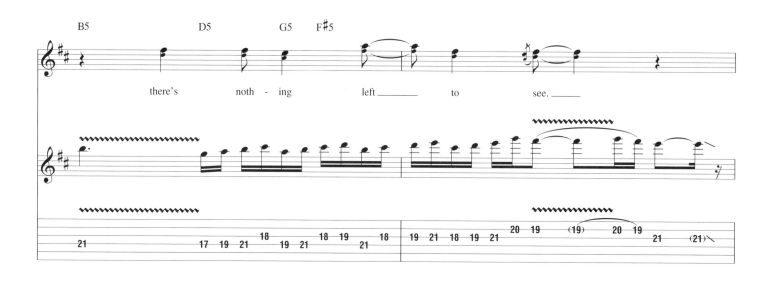

there's noth - ing left ____ to see. ____

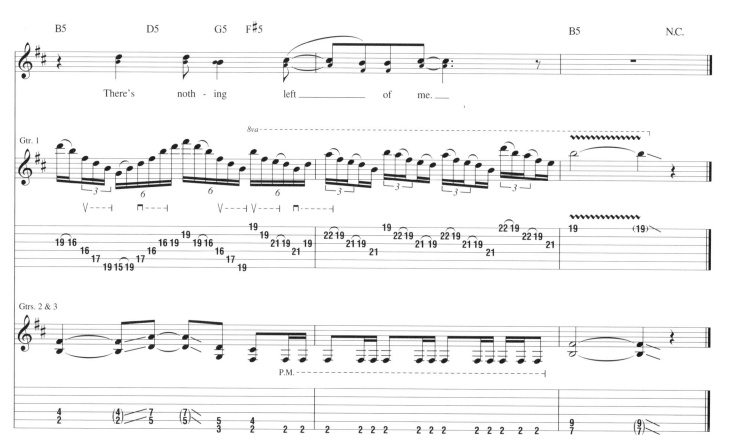

There's noth - ing left ____ of me. ____

Wrecker

Words and Music by Dave Mustaine

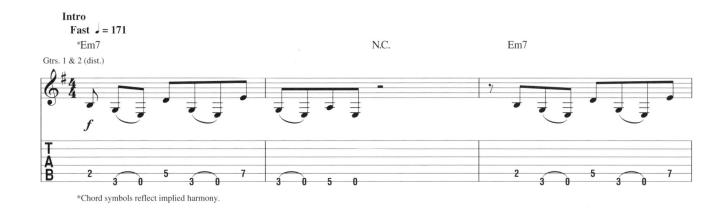

*Chord symbols reflect implied harmony.

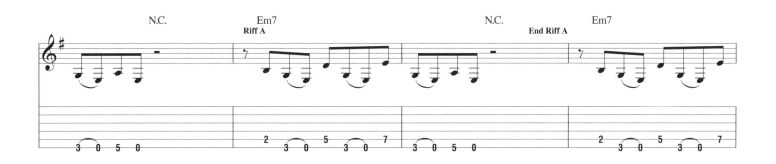

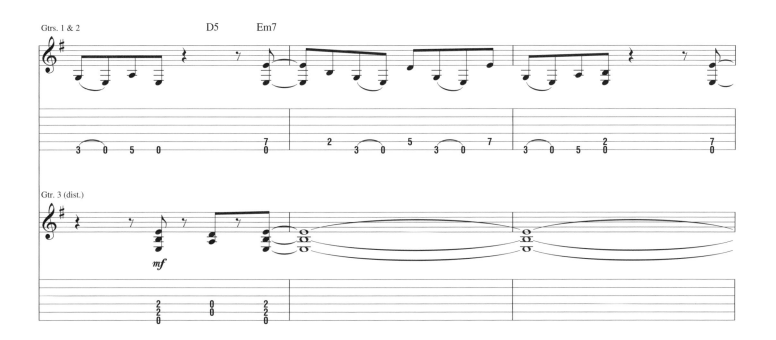

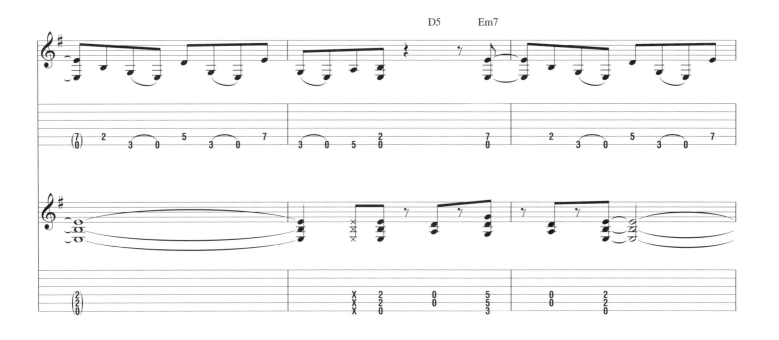

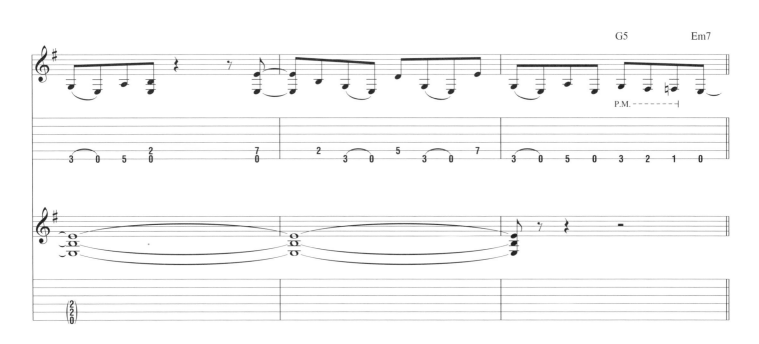

Verse

Gtr. 3 tacet

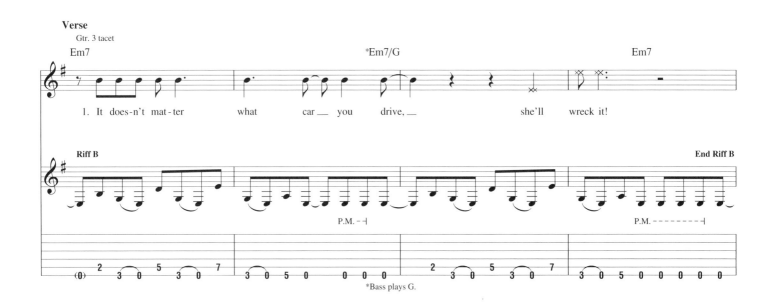

1. It does-n't mat-ter what car __ you drive, __ she'll wreck it!

*Bass plays G.

Verse

Gtr. 1: w/ Riff B (3 times)
Gtr. 2: w/ Riff B

Gtr. 4 tacet

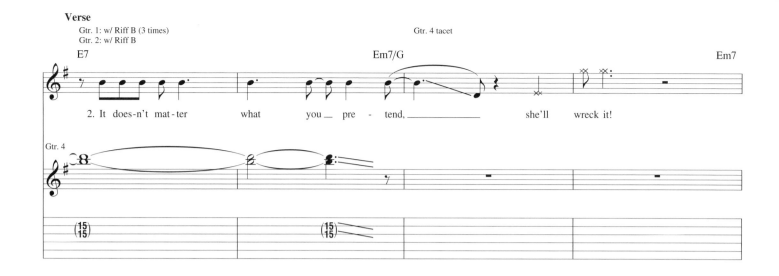

2. It does-n't mat-ter what you pre-tend, she'll wreck it!

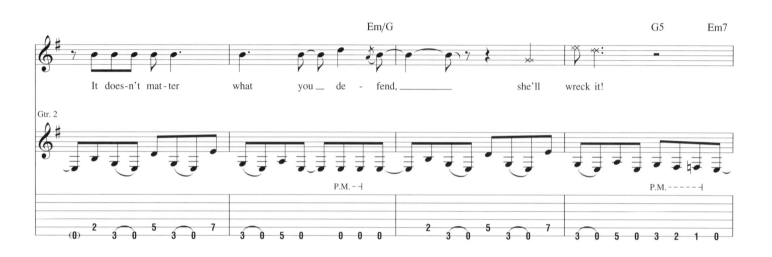

It does-n't mat-ter what you de-fend, she'll wreck it!

Gtr. 2: w/ Riff B

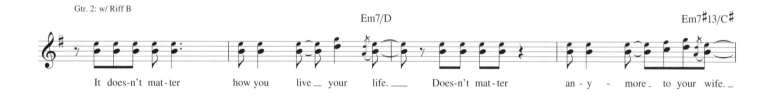

It does-n't mat-ter how you live your life. Does-n't mat-ter an-y - more to your wife.

Gtrs. 1 & 2: w/ Riff C

Does-n't mat-ter e - ven how you die, she'll wreck that too.

Pre-Chorus

Gtrs. 1 & 2: w/ Rhy. Fig. 1

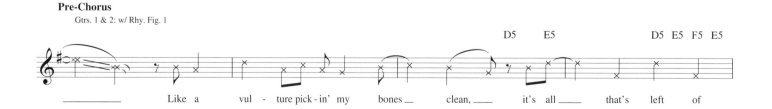

Like a vul - ture pick-in' my bones clean, it's all that's left of

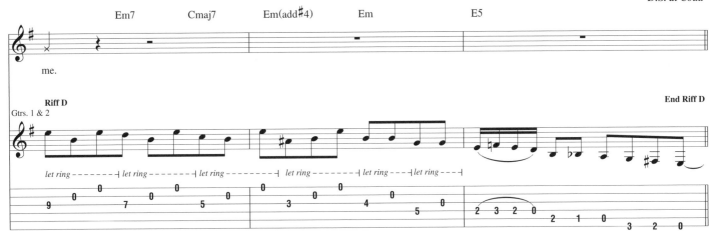

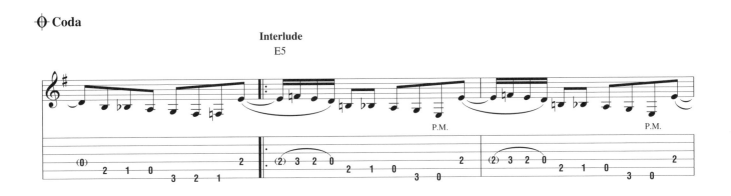

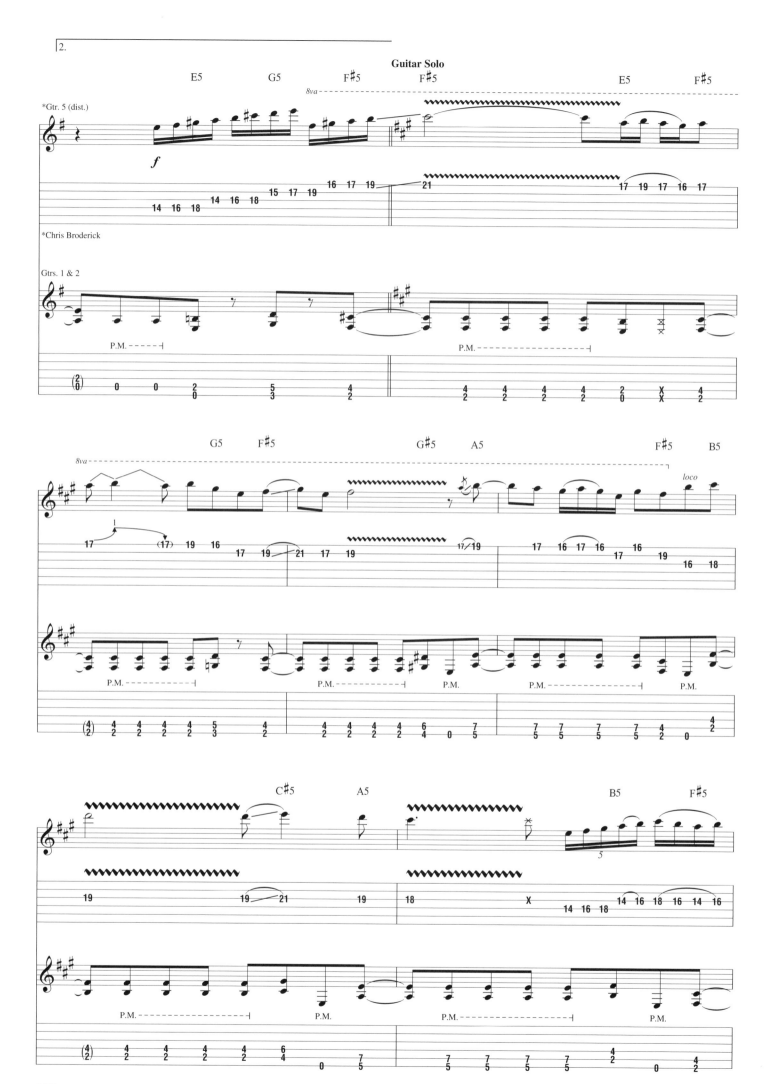

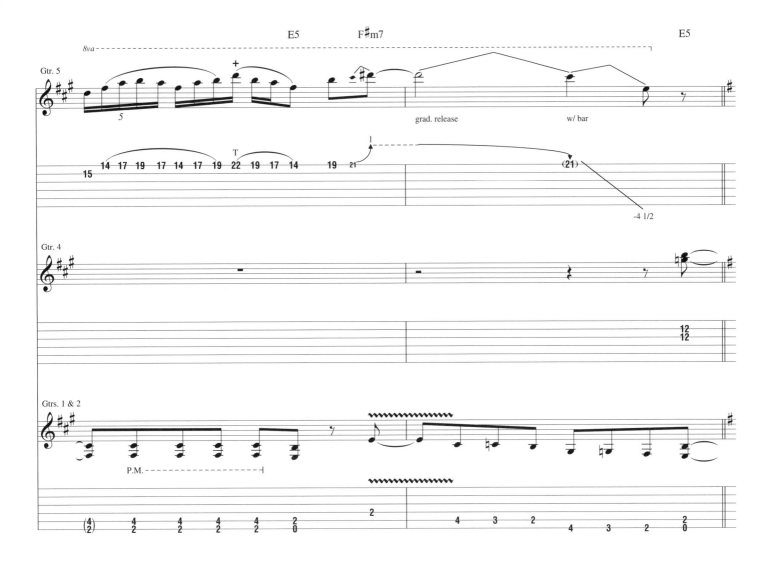

Guitar Solo
Gtr. 5 tacet

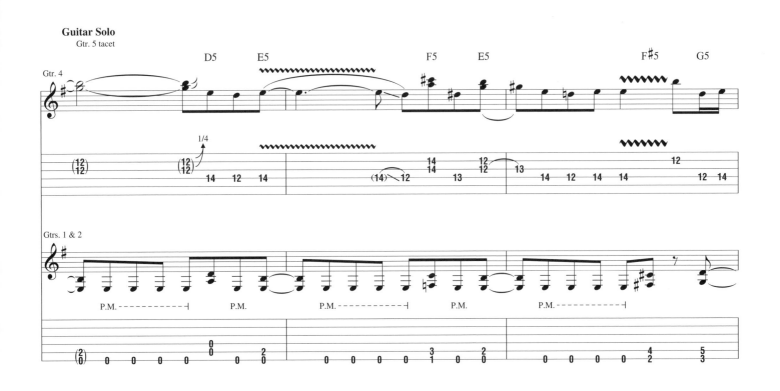

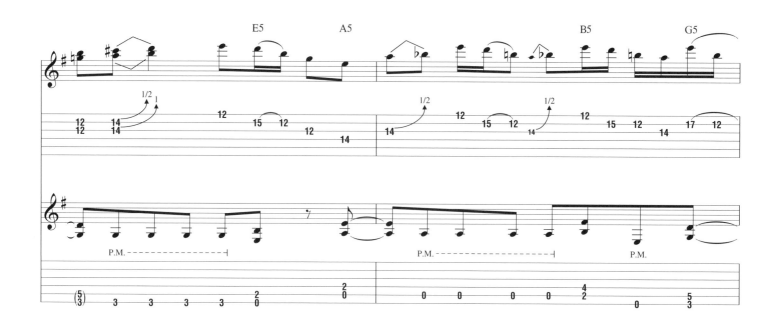

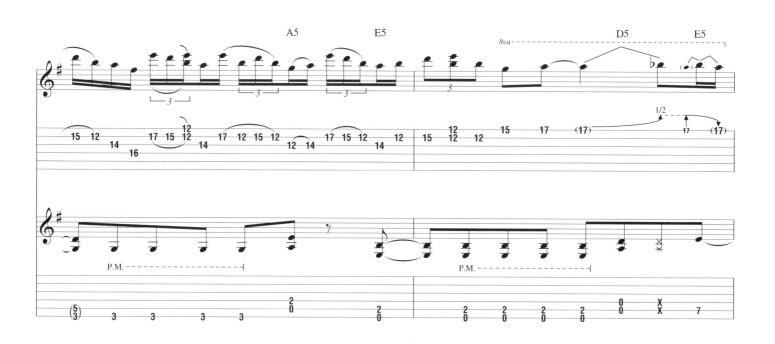

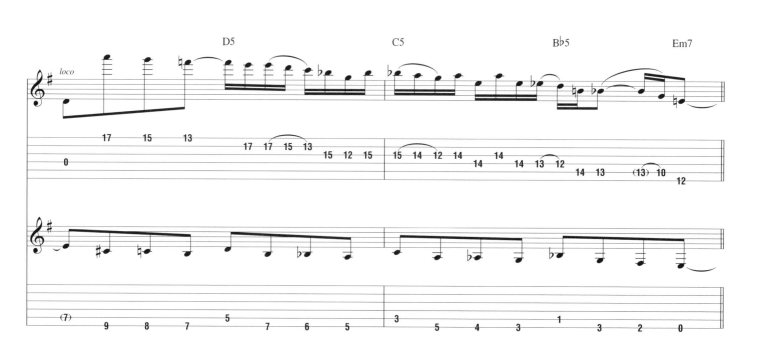

Verse

Gtrs. 1 & 2: w/ Riff B (1 1/2 times)

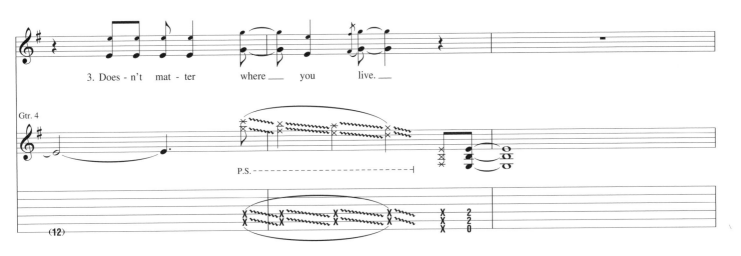

3. Does - n't mat - ter where you live.

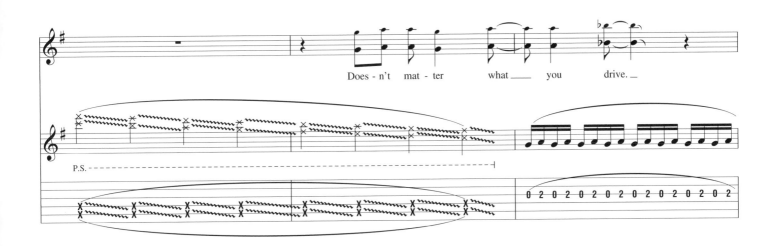

Does - n't mat - ter what you drive.

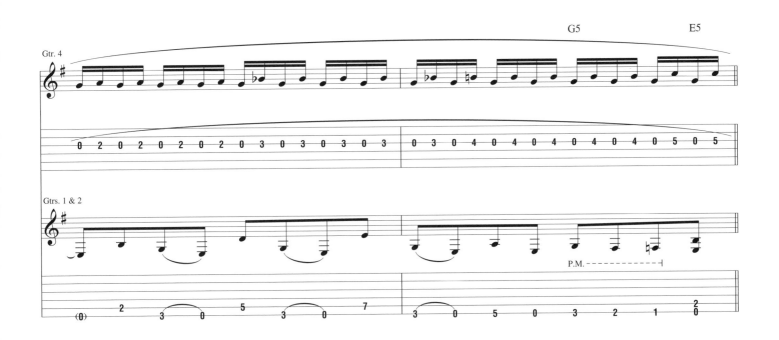

Pre-Chorus

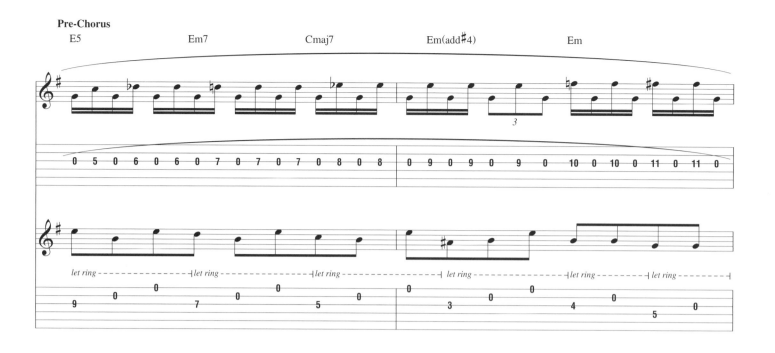

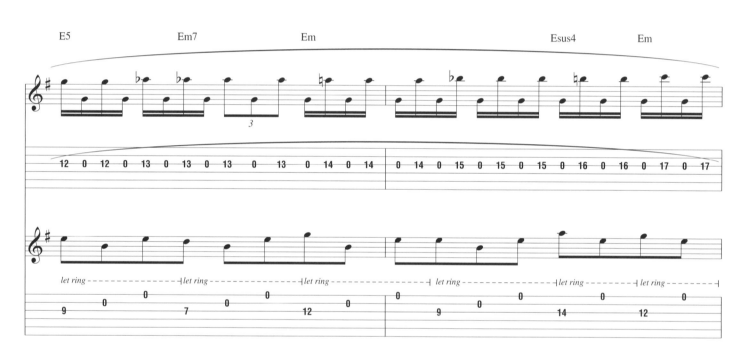

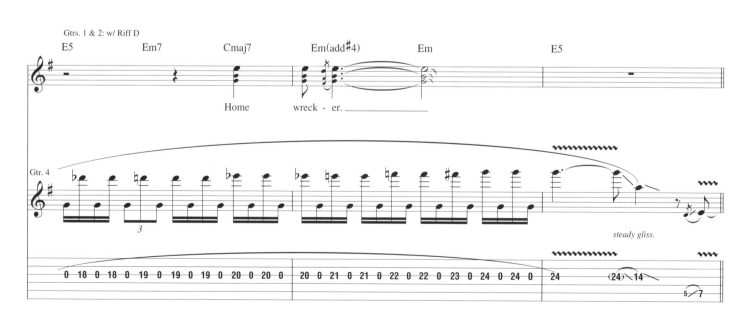

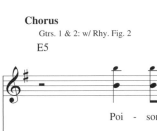

Chorus

Gtrs. 1 & 2: w/ Rhy. Fig. 2

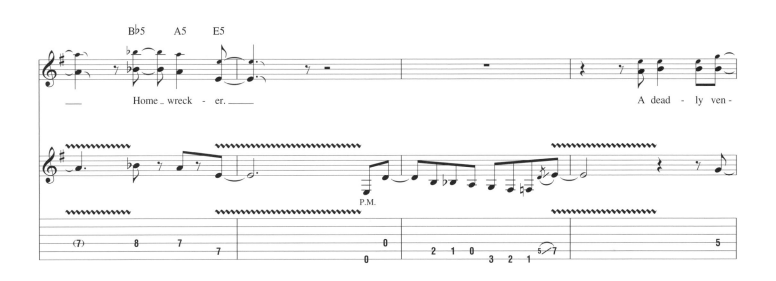

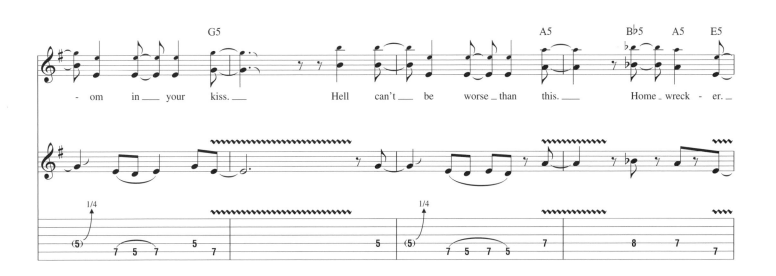

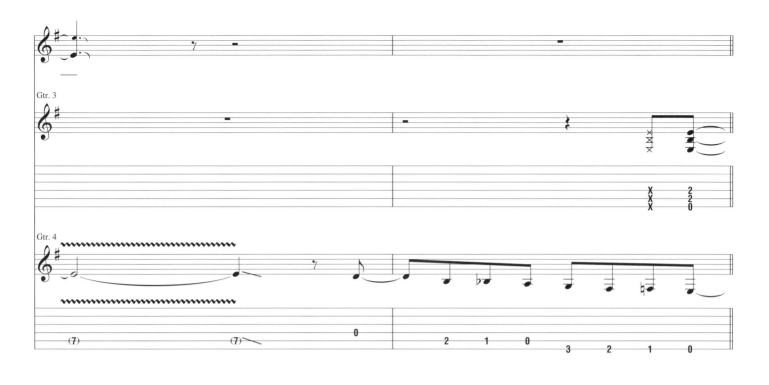

Gtr. 3

Gtr. 4

Outro

Gtrs. 1 & 2: w/ Riff A (4 times)

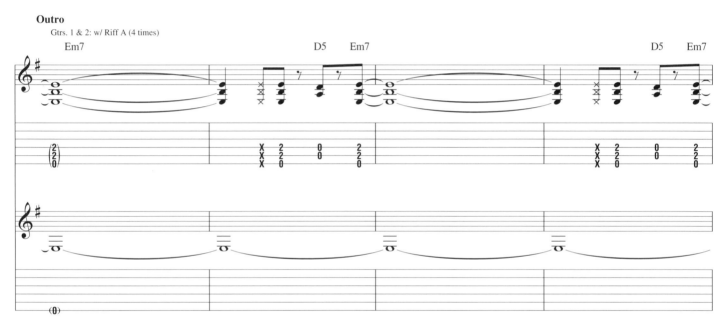

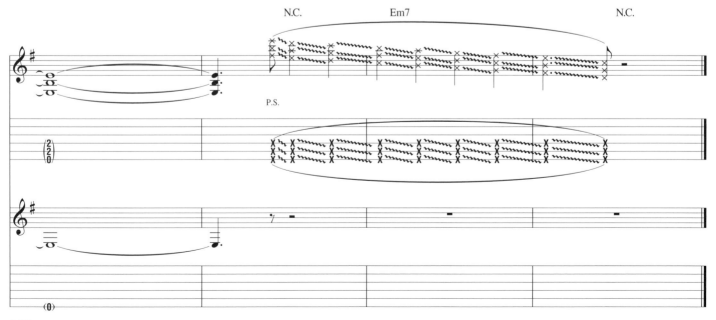

Millenium of the Blind

Words and Music by Dave Mustaine and Marty Friedman

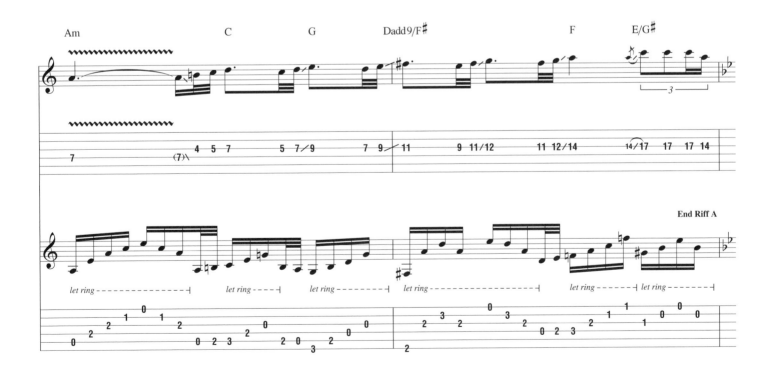

Blind fol - low, blind lead.

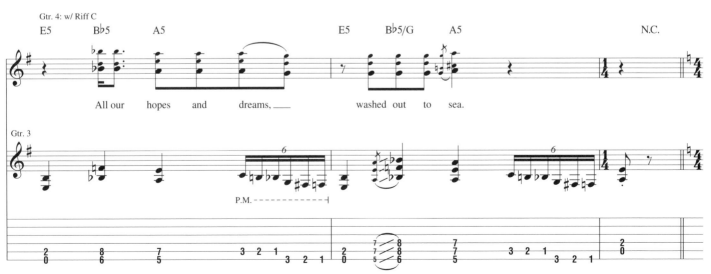

All our hopes and dreams, ___ washed out to sea.

All our hopes and dreams, ___ washed out to sea.

Bridge

Spoken: At the start of time, man-y cen-tu-ries a-go, came the spawn-ing of Christ and the An-ti-christ and dark-ness fell up-on our peo-ple.

And the chil-dren, they were born _ face-less.

With-out eyes, _ they could not see.

Born un - to them-selves, they lived and they died in the mil-len-ni-um of the blind.

Gtr. 2

Gtr. 3

Gtr. 6

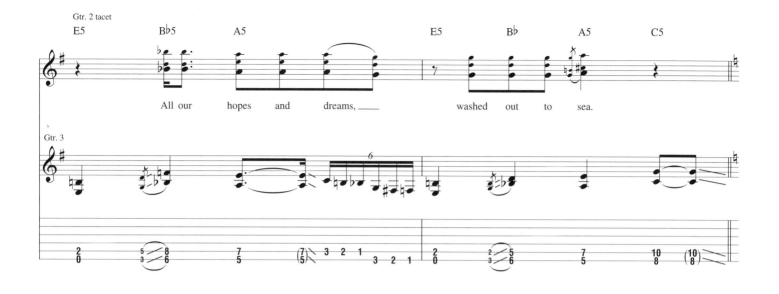

All our hopes and dreams, _____ washed out to sea.

Outro

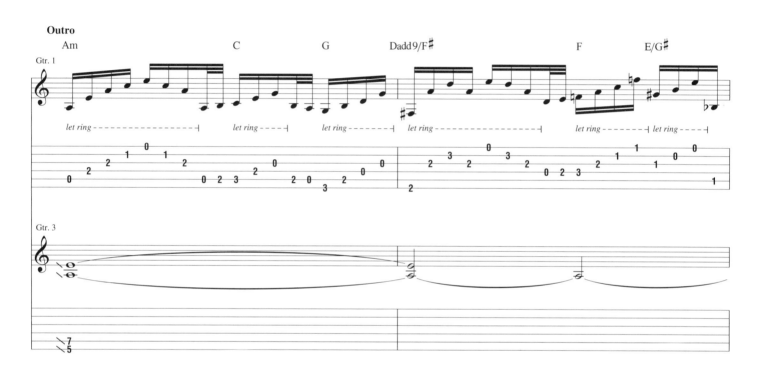

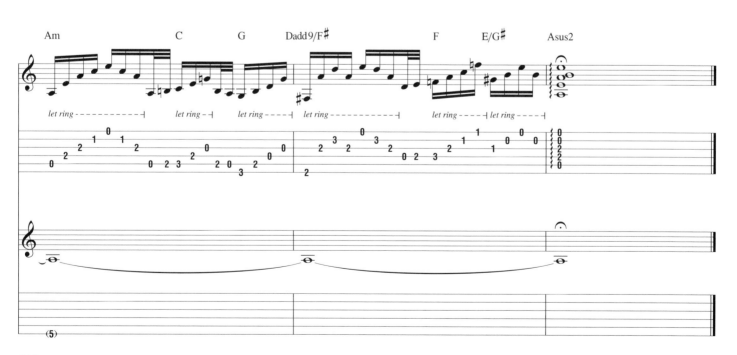

Deadly Nightshade

Words and Music by Dave Mustaine

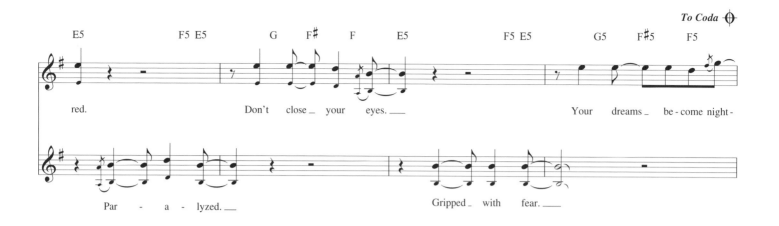

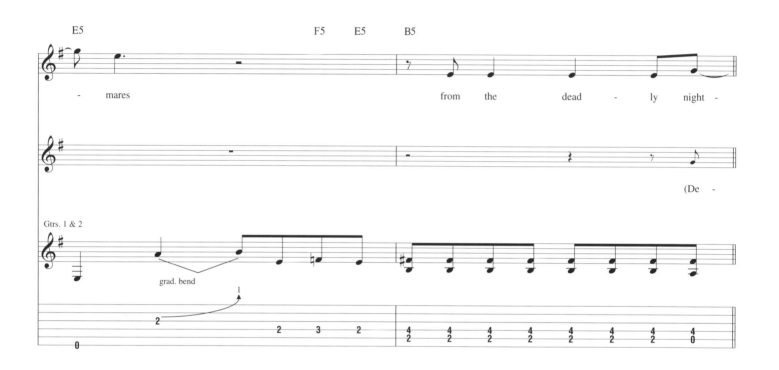

136

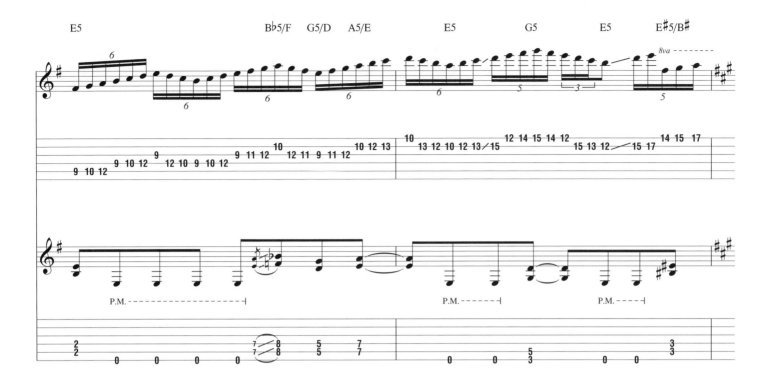

Gtr. 5 tacet

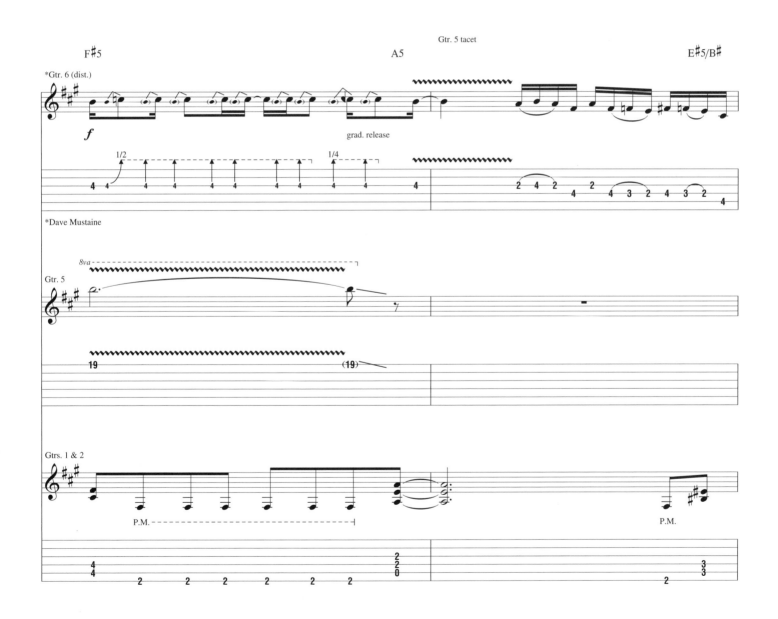

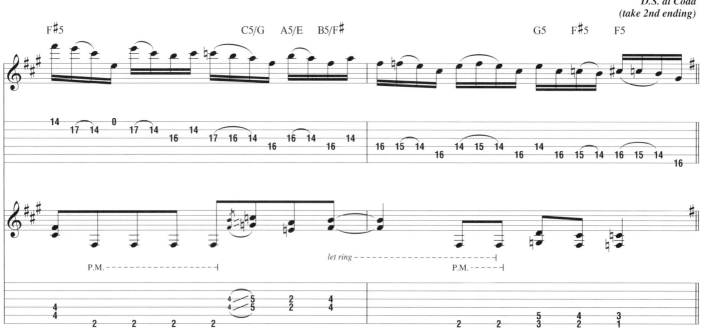

✠ Coda

-mares   from   the   dead   -   ly   night-

Outro-Guitar Solo

Gtr. 1: w/ Riff C (4 times)
Gtr. 2: w/ Riff C (2 times)

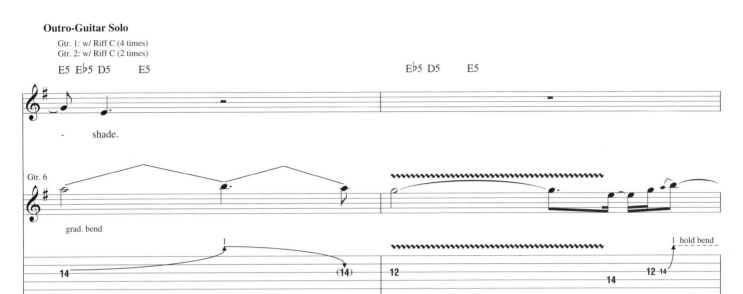

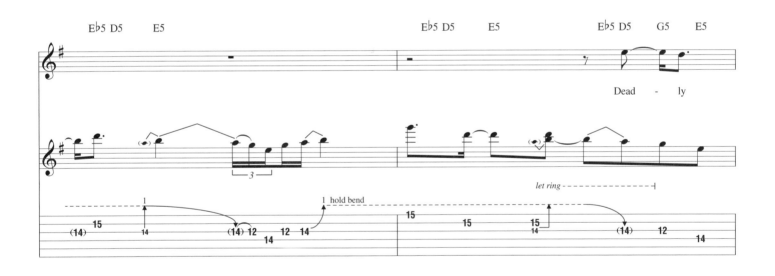

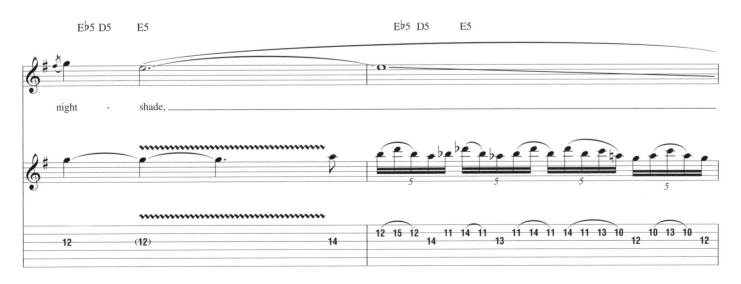

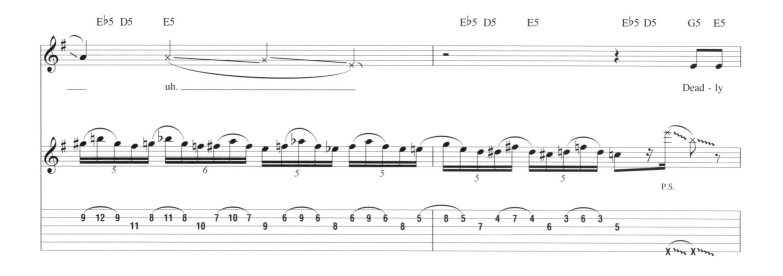

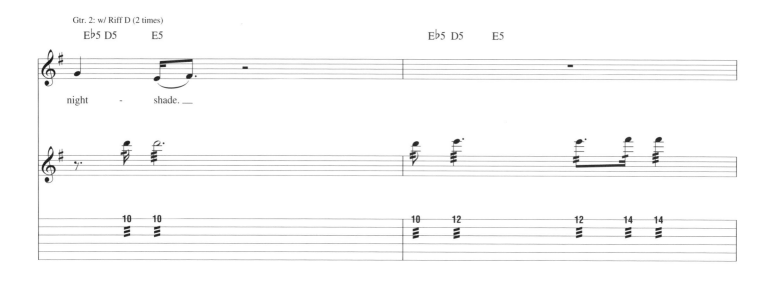

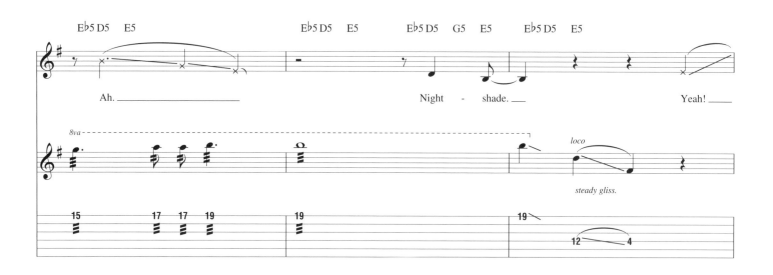

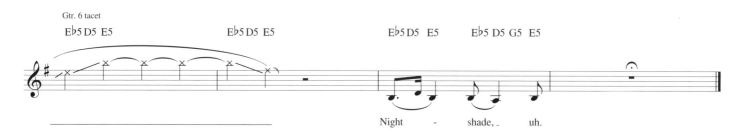

13

Words and Music by Dave Mustaine and John Karkazis

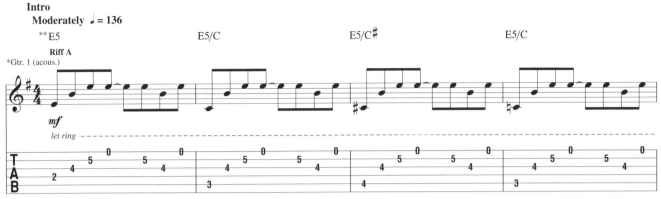

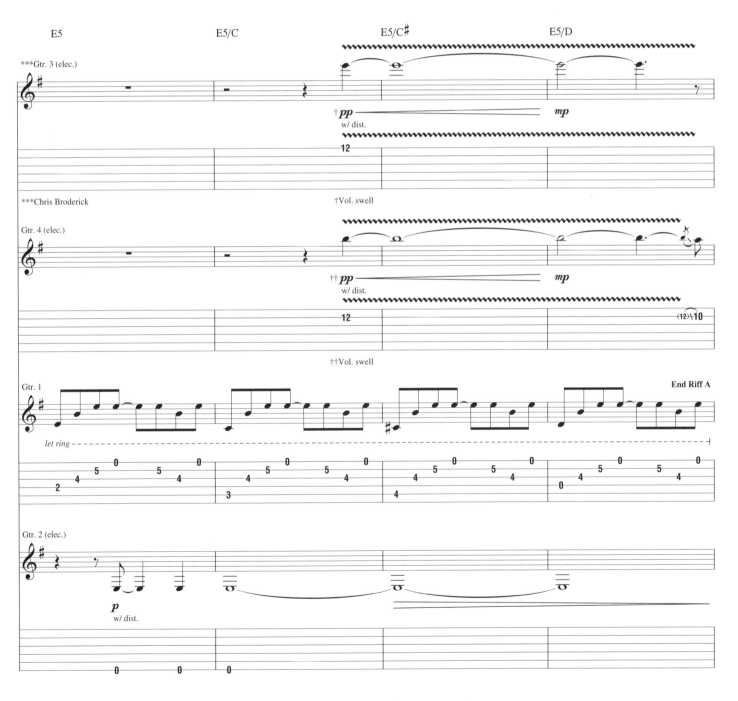

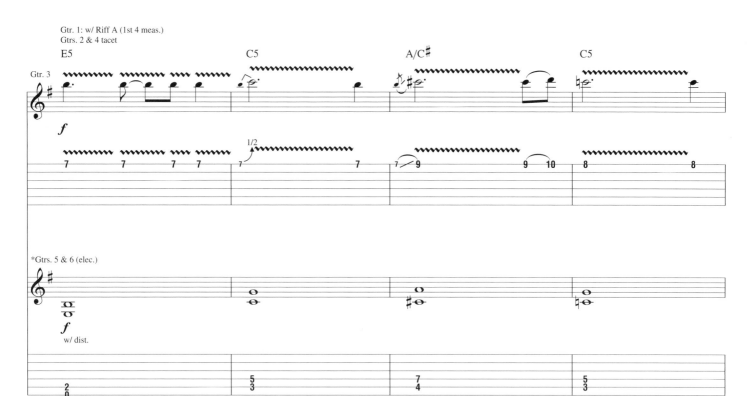

*Composite arrangement

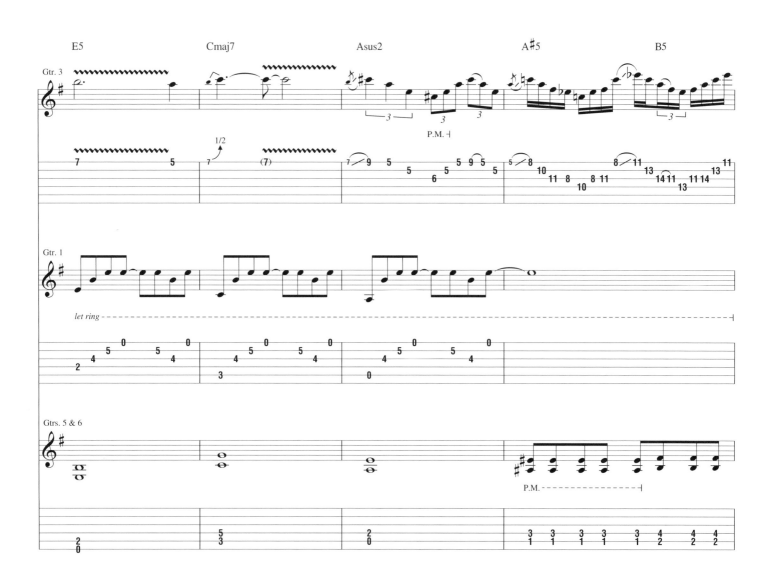

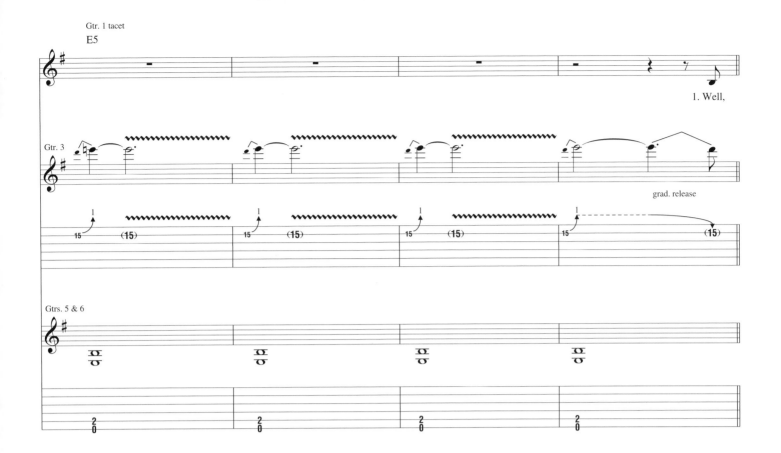

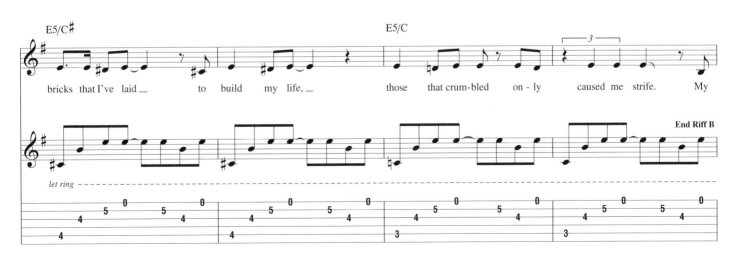

Verse
Half-time feel

thir - teen, I start - ed down this path. Fueled with an - ger, mu - sic was my wrath.

Years of claw - ing at scars that nev - er healed. Drown - ing my mind, the thoughts are too real.

Pre-Chorus
Gtrs. 5 & 6: w/ Riff D

Be - cause I've lived, how man - y times do I have to die?

Be - cause I've lived, ___ how man - y lives ___ do I have to die? ___

Coda

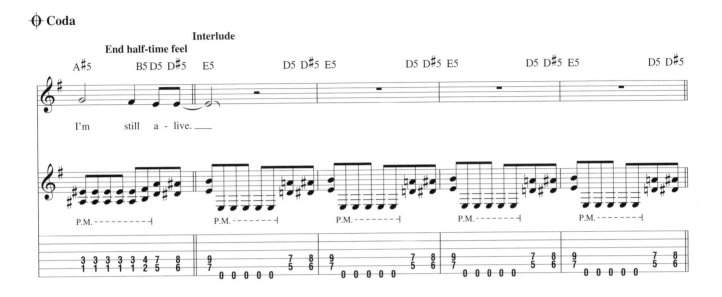

Bridge
Half-time feel

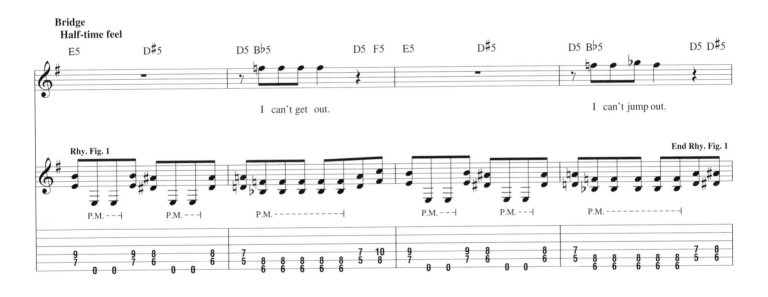

Guitar Solo

Gtrs. 5 & 6: w/ Rhy. Fig. 1 (2 times)

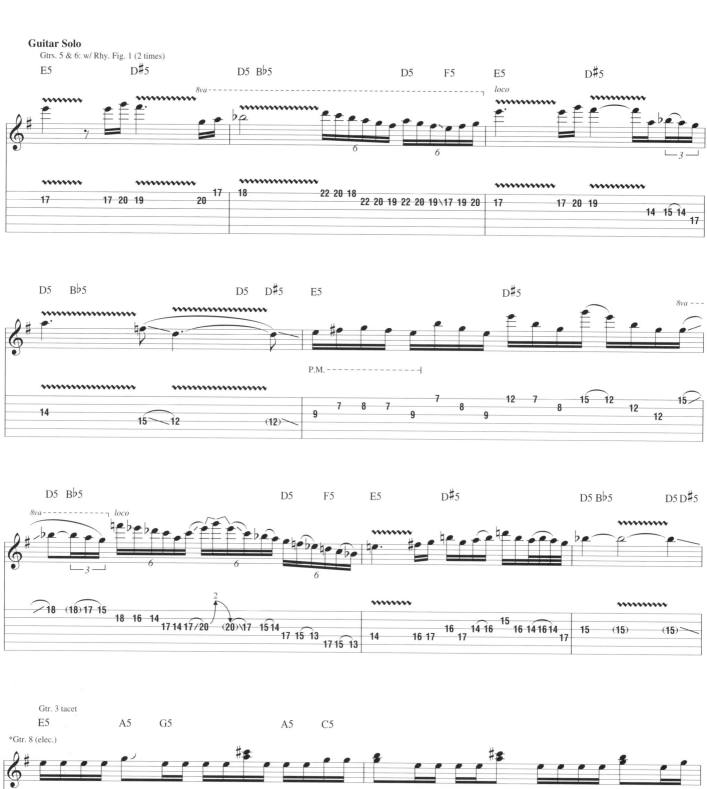

Gtr. 3 tacet

*Gtr. 8 (elec.)

*Dave Mustaine

Rhy. Fig. 2

Gtrs. 5 & 6

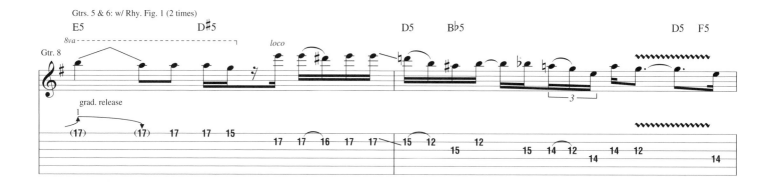

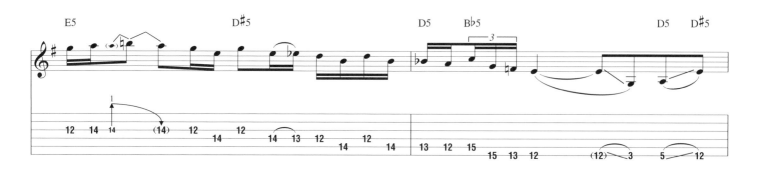

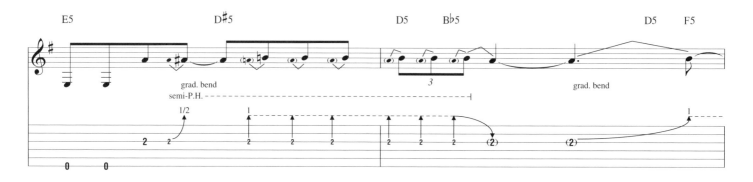

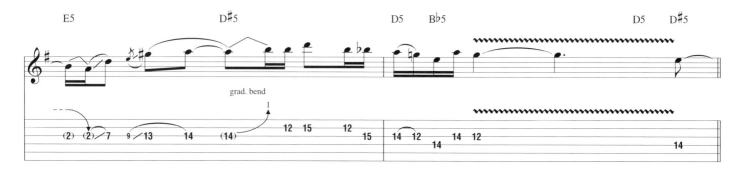

Pre-Chorus

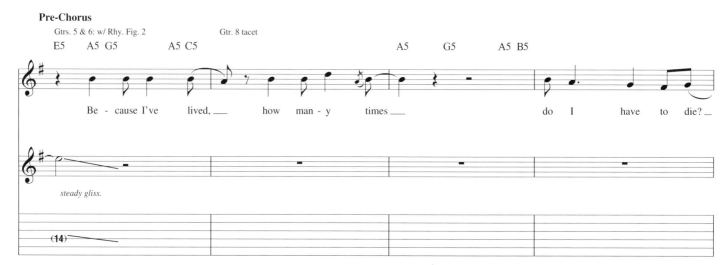

Be - cause I've lived, ___ how man - y times ___ do I have to die? ___

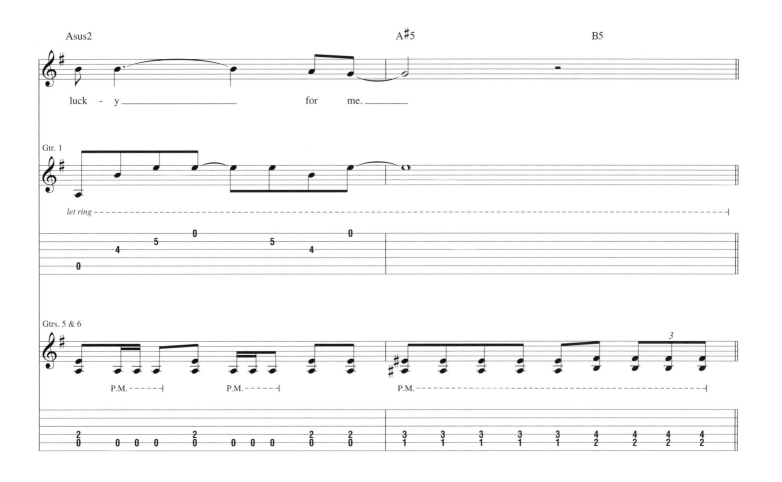

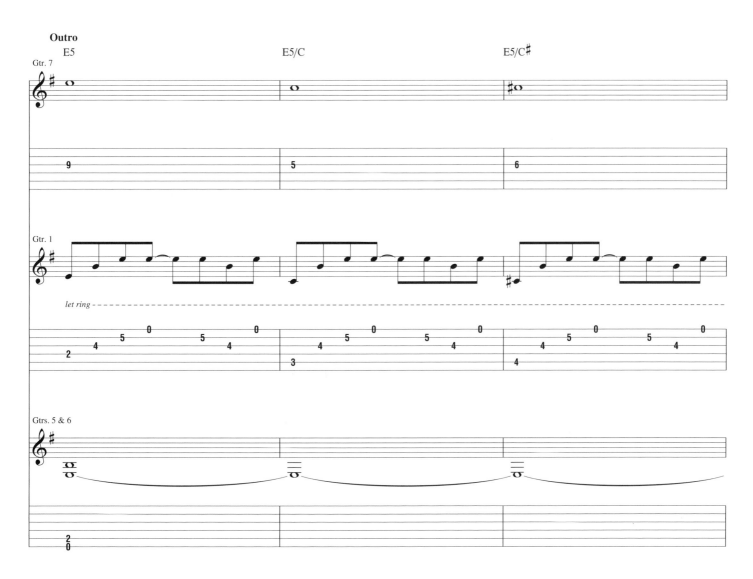

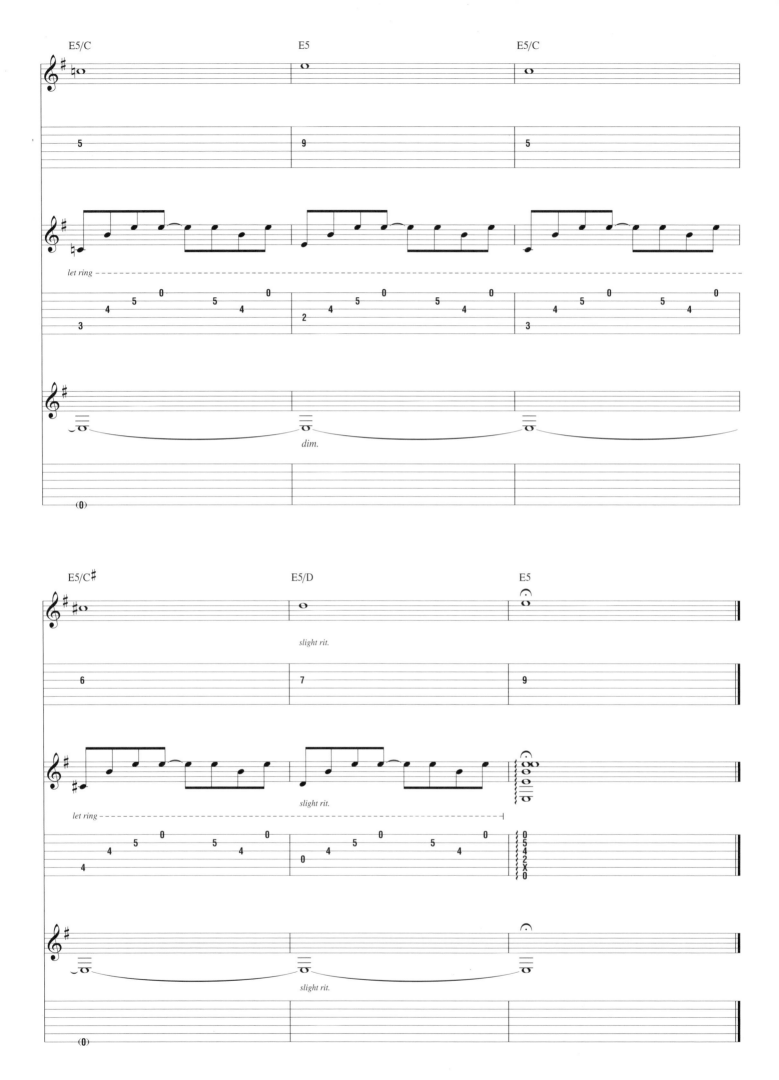